The Civic Renewal Movement

D1558819

Community-Building and Democracy in the United States

Carmen Sirianni
Lewis A. Friedland

© 2005 by the Charles F. Kettering Foundation

ALL RIGHTS RESERVED

For information about permission to reproduce selections
from this book, write to:
        Permissions
        Kettering Foundation Press
        200 Commons Road
        Dayton, Ohio 45459

This book is printed on acid-free paper
First edition, 2005
Manufactured in the United States of America
Library of Congress Cataloging-in-Publication Data

        The Civic Renewal Movement:
        Community-Building and Democracy in the
        United States
        p. cm.
        Includes bibliographical reference
        ISBN 0-923993-13-4

Contents

Introduction

A civic renewal movement to revitalize democracy in the United States has emerged over the past decade. By working to renew and modernize our civic and institutional infrastructure, this movement seeks to foster self-government in the broadest sense. Civic renewal entails more than reforming elections and campaign finance, increasing voting, or making our system more inclusive of the great diversity of Americans. To be sure, these are unfinished projects that warrant much attention. But civic renewal also entails investing in civic skills and organizational capacities for public problem solving on a wide scale and designing policy at every level of the federal system to enhance the ability of citizens to do the everyday work of the republic.

The civic renewal movement—alternatively the "democracy movement," "community-building movement," "civil society movement," or "communities movement"—builds upon the work of activists and innovators in many different arenas. Watershed associations engage various stakeholders in water-quality monitoring, collaborative planning, and hands-on restoration of complex ecosystems, often with the support of innovative state and federal policy. In many low-income communities, congregations work together in ecumenical, faith-based community coalitions that partner with business leaders and educators for school reform and state-of-the-art job training. Neighborhood associations, often organized into citywide systems with substantial funding and staff support from local government, engage in community planning, dispute resolution, crime control, and the hands-on design and construction of public space and public art. In an increasing number of cities, youth commissions involve teens in problem solving and policy development with mayors, city councils, municipal agencies and, indeed, neighborhood associations. Healthy community coalitions bring together civic groups, hospitals, and public health agencies for health education and empowerment among under-served populations. Colleges and universities, as well as K–12 schools, provide an ever-increasing number of service-learning opportunities to renew civic education and contribute directly to community development and environmental restoration.

Our research over the past decade convinces us that, despite many worrisome signs in American civic life, a substantial amount of civic innovation that can inform broad renewal strategies is occurring. It is true, as some argue, that we should concern ourselves with long-term declines in civic engagement and recognize that we have a long, hard road ahead. But it is also true that Americans' capacity to innovate has been demonstrated time and again even amid aggregate declines, and we need to find ways to learn from these innovations and leverage them for democratic revitalization on a much wider scale.

Our research indicates that much of this innovation is of a piece. Many common themes and practices are emerging across distinct arenas. These innovations develop in response to the perceived limits of the usual ways of doing business, whether in revitalizing neighborhoods, restoring watersheds, or improving health. In many instances, innovators borrow from best practices in other arenas and justify their work by appealing to the lively public and scholarly discourse about social capital, civil society, and deliberative democracy. If we look more deeply, we often see a shared vocabulary, despite much variation in practice. Common terms include "relationship building," "consensus seeking," "community asset mapping," "collaborative problem solving," "community visioning," "coproduction," "public work," and "community-building."

In some cases, self-identified movements within specific arenas envision themselves as transforming basic paradigms and practices in their fields. Thus, we see a "watershed movement" that emphasizes place-based and citizen-driven approaches to protecting ecologically integrated watersheds, as well as an over-lapping "community forestry movement" and a "grassroots ecosystem management movement" that insist on the need for collaborative governance of natural resource systems. These movements challenge not only unilateral corporate power but also command-and-control, pollutant-by-pollutant regulation favored by many Washington-based environmental groups. The "environmental justice movement" adds a further challenge by insisting on the empowerment of poor and minority communities, albeit with an increasing emphasis on collaborative problem solving to prevent pollution and reduce risk. These movements bring a renewed civic dynamism to the larger environmental movement and new tools for accomplishing what the usual forms of regulation often cannot.

We see similar movements to revitalize and modernize core institutional and professional practices in other arenas. The self-described "movement to renew the civic mission of higher education" develops new models of service learning and community-university partnership that actively involve students, faculty, administrators, and staff in the work of broad community development. The "community youth development movement" engages young people in creative civic action through 4-H clubs, YMCAs, youth commissions, and myriad other youth groups, while the movement to renew the civic mission of K–12 schools combines teaching principles of constitutional democracy with service learning and other opportunities for active engagement in communities and school governance. Responding to the distinct gender concerns of youth, the "new girls movement" empowers girls and young women through YWCAs and school groups to create safe spaces, free of violence and intimidation, and to contribute to community development through ethnic and tenant associations. In the arena of public safety, the "community policing movement" and broader "community justice movement" aim to transform the practices of professionals in creating safe communities in partnership with citizens who help define problems and implement solutions. The "healthy communities movement" engages community organizations as vital coproducers of health in partnership with traditional professional, public health, and medical institutions. Tens of thousands of citizens have been trained to resolve disputes through collaborative problem solving as part of the "community mediation movement"; its local centers and institutes work with a broad range of other civic organizations. The "civic journalism movement" has generated new professional and organizational practices to enable citizens to deliberate and problem solve more democratically. In addition, the "information commons movement" is inventing ways to use new technological and information capacities as a common-pool resource for community problem solving and the creation of a democratic commonwealth. Many who use diverse methods of structured citizen dialogue for developing informed public opinion and policy consider themselves to be part of a burgeoning "deliberative democracy movement."

The civic renewal movement attempts to weave these various movements and innovations into a larger tapestry that can enable democratic work to become broader and deeper, as well as more complementary and sustainable, in the decades ahead. Without a broad movement linking democratic work across institutional systems, innovation may progress in some arenas but will likely stall or remain invisible in others and fail to inspire action on the scale needed to revitalize our democracy. Unless we can bring these discrete movements and leadership networks into a

*more dynamic relationship with each other, it is unlikely that we will
be able to counter those powerful institutional and cultural forces
in our society that tend to undermine citizen power and capacity for
self-government.*

The civic renewal movement's leaders and theorists have
emerged from innovative organizations within all these arenas.
They have elaborated and exchanged new vocabularies of civic
practice *across* various arenas and networks, for example, from
assets-based community development and community visioning
to environmental justice and community forestry. In doing so,
they have contributed to the development of a "social movement
frame," which scholars have increasingly come to view as critical
to the development of movements. Of course, not all or even most
of those active in innovative community-building networks identify explicitly with a broad civic renewal movement at this point
or share a fully common vocabulary or set of practices. This is
not unusual, however, in the history of social movements, which
almost never begin with a well-defined identity or widely accepted label. Rather, social movements emerge over years, even
decades, from many forms of local action that only gradually—
and often begrudgingly—begin to use a common language and
form broader networks. Even then, they almost never fully eliminate contentious internal struggles over identity and mission,
not to mention favored practices and policies. This pattern holds
for the civil rights, women's, and environmental movements of
recent decades, for the labor movement over the course of a century, and, indeed, for movements of all kinds around the world.
The civic renewal movement is not exceptional in this regard.

To include varied renewal initiatives under the rubric of a
"movement" is an analytic choice, as well as a political argument.
In this book, we will draw on the analytic concepts of social
movement theory to clarify why it makes sense to think in terms
of an emergent movement with an increasingly shared identity.

We will also analyze the ways in which the civic renewal movement distinguishes itself from recent "rights" and "justice" movements, even as it builds on their achievements and maintains many linkages with them.

But in addition to empirical and conceptual analysis, we also make a political argument about why it is critical to build a civic renewal movement with a common identity that cuts across many distinct forms of civic innovation and links diverse networks engaged in public problem solving. *Naming this movement, we hope, will help it flourish.*

The movement, we will argue, should remain pluralistic and nonpartisan, open to learning from a wide array of approaches and to collaborating with elected officials of various political persuasions who are willing to problem solve with citizens. We recognize that many civic activists, ourselves included, also maintain specific partisan identities and advocacy agendas that are not shared by others in the civic renewal movement. But people can be partisan Democrats or Republicans and still collaborate to revitalize civic education in our schools, partner with congregations to revitalize neighborhoods, work with traditional adversaries to restore ecosystems, and engage diverse stakeholders in community visioning for an entire city or region. Indeed, citizens not only *can do* these things; they *already are doing* them in many settings that defy neat political categories. Citizens can advocate different agendas regarding a specific set of federal regulations or social programs and still believe that it is possible—indeed indispensable—to remain in dialogue about the civic fundamentals of policy design. They can be deeply committed activists in various rights and justice movements and still be part of a broad civic renewal movement that attempts to enrich community-building practices.

The civic renewal movement seeks to enrich and modernize democratic practice and civic learning so that, in the famous phrase of America's greatest democratic philosopher, John Dewey, democracy becomes "a way of life," not just a "form of government." The civic renewal movement also seeks to enhance "public policy for democracy" so that the design of policy at every level of the federal system enhances citizens' capacities for responsible self-government, rather than treating them merely as passive clients, aggrieved victims, entitled claimants, or consumers ever-ready to use the exit option. *The civic renewal movement does not presume to displace or substitute for all the other ways in which individuals and groups organize, advocate, or protest.* Democracy is much more diverse and raucous than any one movement—even one with very broad purposes, such as the civic renewal movement—can ever hope to encompass.

In the wake of the highly polarized 2004 presidential election, civic collaboration might seem a bit quaint. After all, some would say, activists mobilized very effectively to turn out partisans on the basis of very targeted messages to their respective bases. New political organizations, some tailored specifically to the Internet age, raised enormous sums of money and mobilized volunteers in unprecedented ways. The media portrayal of a country bifurcated into "blue states" and "red states"—and blue and red "states of mind"—leaves little room to imagine citizens collaborating across deep divides of party, policy, even morality.

Yet many scholars and public opinion analysts have cast doubt on this image of a citizenry so deeply polarized on core values. Much of the innovation we portray in this book points to a citizenry that is often very pragmatic in seeking ways to work across various divisions in the interest of a larger public or community good. The vitality of our democracy, we argue, depends on our capacity to nurture these and many other forms of civic collaboration, even as we will undoubtedly do battle on some critical policies, prefer different parties to represent our interests and ideals, and mobilize vigorously through various other movements and organizations. Broad democratic self-governance in a complex world is simply not possible without expanding the fields of innovative civic collaboration. The election of 2004 polarized—and in some ways impoverished—our imagination of how citizens can contribute to the everyday work of our republic and make democracy a way of life. But it also demonstrated how much we need forms of civic collaboration that are distinct from the new forms of political mobilization.

The civic renewal movement faces many barriers, to be sure, and has no guarantee that it will transform American civic and political life. Innovative civic practice confronts serious obstacles within each institutional and policy arena in the form of entrenched bureaucratic, corporate, political, and professional practices and distributions of power. Some general social and cultural trends erode community connections and civic engagement, thus making a broad movement that much more difficult to build. A movement that foregrounds collaborative problem solving and democratic deliberation does not have available the same tactical repertoires (such as mass protests, sit-ins, and freedom rides) that have enabled various rights and justice movements, or fundamentalist values-based movements, to galvanize the public on a broad scale. While innovations have spread in most arenas we have examined, in several they have stalled and a number of important networks have been disbanded. In addition, an increasingly polarized political climate that so fiercely mobilizes partisans for rhetorical and electoral victory can too easily displace the ethos and investments needed to engage citizens in genuine problem solving and deliberation. Thus, while civic innovations and movements inspire optimism and generate hope in the capacity of citizens to reclaim their democracy, they also face very serious challenges in political culture and institutional practice.

In Part One we begin by examining some innovative models and movements operating in distinct arenas. This will not only provide a broad landscape but will also help clarify why civic innovation is occurring. In some cases, innovation has been proceeding with several decades of capacity building and policy design; in others, with much less. We group various models and organizations under several broad rubrics, though we also recognize that there are fuzzy boundaries, many overlaps, and even more varied approaches than we can capture in a short book. We also provide a selection of case profiles. There are other forms of civic and political engagement and advocacy vital to democracy that are not included here because they have not—or have not yet—made creative linkages to the kinds of community-building or civic problem-solving methodologies that are our central focus. We include the following approaches:

- Community organizing and development
- Civic environmentalism
- Engaged campus
- Community youth development and K–12 civic education
- Healthy communities
- Public journalism and civic communications

In Part Two we examine some of the contours of the civic renewal movement as such. In particular, we explore the general factors driving innovation and the contributions a broad movement promises to make beyond its separate parts. We look at various themes in the movement "master frame" and analyze the ways in which it distinguishes itself from the frames of "rights" and "justice" movements, even as it might nonetheless enrich and complement them. Frames, by nature, are dynamic, contested, and porous; they are not fixed sets of neatly arranged components. Any presentation (especially a relatively abbreviated one) is necessarily selective and inexact. Ours draws directly on the civic innovations and movements we profile in Part One, as well as upon a diverse array of framing documents (declarations, sets of principles, and theoretical works) that articulate core themes. We proceed inductively from these. We also draw on our interviews with more than 700 innovators, as well as from a series of national strategy conferences we hosted with leaders from various fields. Our configuration of frame components undoubtedly reflects our own analytic proclivities, as well as our relationships to the various leaders and organizations with whom we have collaborated in various movement-building projects. Engaged scholarship has opened up windows on the movement that would otherwise have been unavailable to us, yet it positions us in distinct ways toward specific ideas and practices. Others in the movement might configure the frame differently in some ways, for instance, emphasizing "community service" instead of "coproduction of public goods," foregrounding "social justice" rather than "democracy," or highlighting "volunteerism" rather than "civic professionalism" and "institutional culture change." A robust framing process welcomes such dynamism and disagreement.

In Part Three we consider various movement-building initiatives of the past decade and the extent to which these initiatives have laid the foundations for a broad movement linking diverse networks *across* arenas. The accomplishments to date have been important ones, but the limits have also been evident. We analyze several critical challenges that a broad civic renewal movement faces in establishing itself as a recognized and consequential movement in American civic and political life. Because the movement invariably must grapple with political parties in its attempts to change the operative frames of politics and to open up new opportunities for innovative institutional practice and policy design, we discuss the relationship between partisanship and nonpartisanship in the movement and several

clusters of ideas within the two major parties that are most
congruent with civic renewal.

Finally, in Part Four we provide an overview of our own
research (and research debts), as well as an annotated selection
of scholarly resources on which we have drawn. We also include
a selection of important civic declarations, practical tool kits,
compendia of stories and case studies, and a list of organizational Web sites central to innovation and movement building.
Because this book is intended primarily for civic leaders, institutional innovators, and everyday citizen activists and students,
as well as those in government, business, and the professions
seeking broader civic purpose and partnership in their work,
we have limited the usual scholarly apparatus to this section.
And while our book provides a conceptual and organizational
map to a very diverse field, citizens can find in this section some
very practical road maps to innovative action and productive
public work. We hope that these maps provide some guidance
for the journey that is democracy.

Part One:

Civic Innovations, Diverse Movements

Community Organizing and Development

Civic Environmentalism

Engaged Campus

Community Youth Development and K–12 Civic Education

Healthy Communities

Public Journalism and Civic Communications

Community Organizing and Development

C ommunity organizing and community development in urban settings take many different forms and include a rich array of networks. The ones we highlight here share the view that mobilizing and advocacy strategies in the old, contentious style pioneered by Saul Alinsky, while often necessary, are not enough. More attention needs to be focused on collaborative problem solving and sustainable partnerships that can bring lasting gains. There has been a great deal of innovation in this arena in recent years, even in organizations founded or inspired by Alinsky. Among the innovative approaches we discuss here are 1) faith-based community organizing; 2) community development and community-building (especially assets-based and comprehensive models); 3) citywide neighborhood association systems; 4) community visioning, study circles, and other models of deliberative democracy; and 5) community policing and community justice.

Faith-Based Community Organizing

Faith-based organizing brings together congregations and often secular organizations (such as unions, schools, neighborhood associations, and community development groups) into an ecumenical, multi-issue, and multiracial coalition that seeks to expand power, especially for low-income communities. Congregations, the core institutional members, pay dues to an interfaith organization—typically a separate 501(c)(3)—that helps support the work of one or several professional organizers. The main task of organizers is leadership development among lay leaders and clergy, as well as members of other institutions, such as parents, teachers, and principals in a school system.

Faith-based community organizing—alternatively called congregation-based organizing, values-based organizing, relational organizing, or institutional organizing by various national networks—uses religious texts and traditions to ground its vision of a just and democratic society and to model ethical leadership. Thus, the story of Moses provides a lesson in developing broad leadership to share responsibility for the otherwise overwhelming task of freeing the people; the call of the prophet Nehemiah to "rebuild the walls of Jerusalem, so that we may no longer suffer disgrace" inspires campaigns for housing and community development. Catholic congregations draw on theological traditions of economic justice and community connectedness. African American Protestant churches tap into deep traditions of deliverance and freedom. White mainstream Protestant churches draw on social gospel traditions. And Jewish congregations employ the concepts of *mitzvah, tsedakah,* and other social justice teachings. In public meetings that bring congregations together, often with public officials, religious language tends to avoid denominational differences and stresses common themes across traditions, such as "because each of us is a child of God, we deserve to live with dignity." Alternately, leaders may invite prayer from three or four denominational traditions at the beginning of a meeting. Unlike some fundamentalist religious organizing, however, faith-based community organizing does not use Scripture to justify specific policy positions or uncompromising moral stances.

A fundamental principle of congregation-based organizing is that issues are chosen to unite rather than divide community members. Thus, certain issues (for example, abortion and gay and lesbian rights) are off the table and left to other groups to pursue.

Issues are never defined in terms of racial or ethnic identity. Much work goes into building bridges among predominantly white, African American, or Hispanic congregations, including a good deal of outreach to new immigrants and those outside Judeo-Christian traditions currently most receptive to this form of organizing. This broad faith-based approach to community organizing accounts for its substantially greater capacity to mobilize communities and achieve policy success than race-based organizing approaches that highlight special identities of racial oppression. And while social justice remains a central theme, faith-based organizing does not frame issues in ways that are class polarizing. Suburban congregations have increasingly joined with urban ones in broad metropolitan organizations.

Faith-based organizing builds power by first building relationships within and across congregations, especially through one-on-one conversations designed to share mutual values, tap into deep passions for justice, articulate genuine self-interests, and uncover the sources of anger that might motivate action. Power is defined as relational and ethical, rather than merely one-way or exploitative, with the broad goal, in the phrase of one major network, to build an "ethical democracy." But this organizing model is nonetheless clear that it is not compassion or altruism that sustain action. Rather, power and self-interest can be mobilized for broad public purposes. Professional "organizers" provide training to develop clergy and lay "leaders," who take the initiative in conducting extensive "one-on-one" campaigns, "house meetings," and other forums to build consensus on an issue agenda, such as housing, school reform, job training, or neighborhood infrastructure improvement.

Organizers teach leaders the skills to negotiate with political, business, and other officials and how to hold all power accountable. Politics, while inspired by deeply held values, is also a pragmatic art of compromise that recognizes the legitimate interests of other stakeholders, including those with whom contentious struggle may be necessary to bring to the table. Nonpartisan by design, faith-based organizations are prepared to challenge, as well as collaborate with, elected officials from both major parties. Some engage in electoral politics, though primarily through voter registration, education, and get-out-the-vote drives when their own issues have been well defined. Holding politicians accountable through "accountability sessions" and "actions" is a central part of their work.

Advocacy, however, is complemented in faith-based organizing by everyday collaboration to improve institutions, such as schools, which requires parents, teachers, and principals to develop new ways of working together. Faith-based organizing also challenges professionals, such as clergy and teachers, to rethink the civic dimensions of their professional roles. As one pastor put it at a meeting in Boston, faith-based organizing rescued him from decades of feeling overwhelmed by the priest-as-therapist role and lent him renewed energy to work with his community in solving problems and restoring collective hope.

Faith-based organizing has grown substantially in recent years. Indeed, growth and sustainability of organizations affiliated with four major national networks have been due in no small measure to their rethinking of some tenets of the classical community organizing model developed by Alinsky from the 1940s through the 1960s, and especially the rooting of this model in a much more profound and principled use of faith traditions and institutions. The four major networks are the IAF (Industrial Areas Foundation), PICO (formerly the Pacific Institute for Community Organization), the Gamaliel Foundation, and DART (Direct Action and Research Training Center). Several other regional networks and local unaffiliated organizations round out the field. These networks transfer lessons among local organizations, recruit new organizers and, most importantly, provide systematic training to local leaders, typically in five-day or ten-day retreats involving several hundred

people from organizations across the country. Faith-based community organizing has many features of a social movement, though many of its leaders eschew this term.

As of 2004, there were 170 faith-based coalitions in 33 states and the District of Columbia, with the highest concentrations in California, Texas, New York, Florida, Illinois, and Ohio. This represents fivefold growth since 1990. The average faith-based community organization has 30 institutional members, with a few having more than 100. The largest to date, United Power for Action and Justice, in metropolitan Chicago, with some 300 member institutions, includes not only religious congregations, but also unions, ethnic associations, neighborhood groups, community health centers, and hospitals. As of 1999, when the most thorough census was taken, some 4,000 institutions were affiliated with faith-based community organizations. Some 2,700 people served on their governing boards, and 24,000 core leaders participated actively at any given time. The networks included some 460 professional organizers. In addition to membership dues, which account for 22 percent of overall funds, and private foundation and corporate grants, which provide another 30 percent, faith-based organizing is supported by the Interfaith Funders network and its member organizations, the largest of which is the Catholic Campaign for Human Development.

Increasingly, these local and metropolitan organizations are cooperating on state and regional levels to achieve policy goals and collaborating out of network with various local stakeholders to develop sustainable partnerships for school reform and job training. The PICO California Project, for instance, worked with the state superintendent of public instruction and the U.S. secretary of education in 1995 to expand school-to-work transition programs for high school youth and later worked successfully to expand after-school programs and primary health care clinics. The Texas IAF, drawing on successful local campaigns and partnerships, developed an Alliance School program at the state level to support educational reform with empowered parents and to transform local school cultures to support the learning of low-income students. The Texas IAF also has campaigned successfully at the state level around utility rates and indigent health care. And it has been able to transfer Project QUEST, its innovative job training initiative in San Antonio, to other cities around the state (see case profile).

Project QUEST

In the face of layoffs and continued labor market restructuring in the 1990s, COPS and Metro Alliance, the two IAF organizations in San Antonio, designed a job-training program to provide guaranteed high-skilled jobs at a living family wage. The design for QUEST (Quality Employment Through Skills Training) emerged from extensive house meetings, conducted by lay leaders from the congregations, during which ordinary low-income workers and welfare recipients told the stories of failed programs and identified the supports they would need to succeed (such as two-year training, coordinated social services, child care, and team building). This grassroots research was complemented by collaborative research with academics and policy analysts, as well as by "research meetings" held with employers and designed to build relationships for further collaboration. Leaders also used their congregational networks to recruit and screen applicants and provide continuing moral support with high expectations for success.

While the struggle to obtain adequate public funding has, at times, been contentious and employers were initially resistant, COPS and Metro Alliance have been able to leverage their power to create what they call a "new social compact" between employers, workers, and the community and to broker significant changes in employers' hiring practices and community college programs for a much wider population than those enrolled in the QUEST training itself. This compact built upon the reserves of trust generated through previous collaboration with employers and bankers on school reform and community development. QUEST graduates have received substantially higher wages than those in other job-training programs. The Texas IAF has been able to transfer the QUEST model to other areas of the state (the Rio Grande Valley, Austin, El Paso, Dallas) and to cities such as Tucson, Arizona, through its southwest network. Some cities have added short-term customized training and, in Tucson, Job Path requires that its graduates pay the program back either financially or through community service.

Community Development and Community-Building

The community development movement, which began in the 1960s, grew slowly in its first decade and a half. Then, in the 1980s, in response to federal housing cuts, the number of nonprofit community development corporations (CDCs) engaged in neighborhood revitalization burgeoned to 2,000. And in the 1990s, with more consistent support from the Clinton administration and the National Community Development Initiative, led by two major community development intermediaries, capacity was further strengthened. The number of CDCs now stands at about 3,600, according to criteria established by the National Congress for Community and Economic Development (NCCED), though the count may be as high as 8,000 by looser standards. With the emergence of broader "community-building" strategies and "comprehensive community initiatives" (see CCRP case profile), many other kinds of neighborhood and youth groups, senior centers and merchants' associations, social service agencies and congregations (distinct from the faith-based model discussed above) have become part of the community development movement. This movement is supported by an elaborate structure of partners and support organizations in the banking and corporate community and local, state, and federal governments as part of the organizational field.

The growth of CDCs has often been propelled by community organizing against bank redlining in African American neighborhoods and discrimination against immigrants and other groups. The grassroots "community reinvestment movement," which has achieved major gains with the Community Reinvestment Act and has helped bring several hundred billion dollars of additional capital to distressed neighborhoods, has increasingly aligned itself with CDCs over the past decade.

As CDCs became professional housing developers, "bricks and mortar" replaced much of their grassroots organizing. Yet many have remained closely allied to community groups and neighborhood protest movements, and some local and state CDC associations have joined faith-based organizing coalitions such as the Greater Boston Interfaith Organization, which boasts 100 member groups. CDCs have often developed tenant management councils and nurtured neighborhood leadership for CDC boards and other community and city agencies. In recent years, organizing and neighborhood leadership development have increased in response to concerns over too much professionalization.

In the past decade, assets-based community development has also helped to revitalize citizen engagement in the field. Developed by John McKnight and John Kretzmann on the basis of lessons from successful community groups, the assets-based model involves the community in mapping and mobilizing assets of all kinds: unrecognized skills, vacant land, underutilized public buildings, innumerable small civic associations, and local purchasing power. Equally important, the assets-based model has provided a profound shift away from a focus on the community's "deficits," in which, to quote John McKnight's apt phrase, "the *citizen* retreats, the *client* advances." The deficits approach, the basis of many social service and professional intervention programs, has had a demoralizing impact on community action. By contrast, the assets approach enables civic and community development groups, with partners in social service and other agencies, to identify and build on strengths and relationships that often go unrecognized.

Thousands, perhaps even tens of thousands, of community groups have used the assets-based model over the past decade. In addition, a substantial number of community foundations, state Extension Services, United Way chapters, settlement houses, healthy community coalitions, youth development groups, public and private agencies, and national foundations that fund health and human service innovations have undergone training to incorporate assets-based development into their work.

At the national level, the Assets-Based Community Development Institute at Northwestern University assists this broad range of groups. The National Community Building Network convenes local social service and community development groups, as well as local and national foundations, to exchange lessons and develop policy. The Development Training Institute provides training and has contributed to the broad theorization of community-building as part of neighborhood revitalization, resident empowerment, and broad civic renewal. The Local Initiatives Support Corporation (LISC), which has assisted in capacity building and financing for more than 2,400 CDCs in 38 cities and for its rural program in 37 states, has also included community policing, community-building, and consensus organizing in some of its recent programming. The Center for Community Change provides community and youth organizing assistance to community development groups in its broad network of partners. The National Congress for Community Economic Development serves as the major trade association for CDCs, with an affiliated network of faith-based community economic development groups that constitute roughly 15 percent of the CDC field. And there are 34 state-level CDC associations, as well as many citywide associations.

The Families and Democracy Project, which draws on faith-based relational organizing and the public work approach of the Center for Democracy and Citizenship at the University of Minnesota, has much in common with assets-based community development. It emerged from a critique of the traditional provider/client model of family services and argues that the work of "strengthening families in our time must be done mostly by families themselves working democratically in local communities," in partnership with neighborhoods, school districts, medical clinics, and religious congregations. In the various initiatives of the Families and Democracy Project, such as Putting Family First and Partners in Diabetes, family therapists work as civic professionals who help develop leadership among networks of families. Putting Families First has now spawned a grassroots movement that aims to enable families to regain control of their children's overscheduled lives in the interest of more family time. The movement has been heralded widely in the press.

CCRP, Inc.

The Comprehensive Community Revitalization Program (CCRP) is recognized by many as a model comprehensive community development initiative. With support from the Surdna Foundation and other foundations and corporate partners in the early 1990s, CCRP has sought to leverage the capacity of four well-established CDCs in the South Bronx. Residents engaged in widespread public involvement through an initial community-visioning process that formulated Quality-of-Life Physical Plans for the neighborhoods. The plans won a 1995 American Planning Association Presidential Award. CCRP provides venture capital and organizational assistance that permits CDCs to generate new initiatives quickly and establish new partnerships strategically, with an ethos of citizens as everyday problem solvers rather than simply as recipients of services.

For instance, the CDCs developed five new family health care practices, a 108-bed residence for AIDS patients, and a home health care enterprise for AIDS/HIV services, based on the experience of one CDC in long-term senior care. They created a Beacon School, with 1,000 youths involved each month in a broad range of cultural, recreational, and community service activities. They also developed a Head Start program with innovative training for home-based child care and initiated a New Bronx Employment Service with job centers in CDC buildings. A men's group provides mutual support to participants seeking employment, and tenant groups organize support for victims of domestic violence. Intergenerational gardens and farmers' markets provide a focus for community-building and exchange. The Health Realization program encourages people to see themselves as problem solvers and community builders rather than as victims. Residents and corporate partners have worked with middle school students to clean up the Bronx River and develop a greenway corridor to the Bronx Zoo. Residents have also collaborated with the police department in creating neighborhood crime watches and safe corridors for school children, while also holding the police accountable.

Neighborhood Associations

Neighborhood associations have existed for many decades in the United States. But since the mid-1970s, in response to local organizing as well as federal models and mandates for community representation (such as Community Action, Model Cities, and

Community Development Block Grants), an increasing number of cities have formally recognized such associations and even funded them as an essential component of local governance, planning, and self-help. By 1984, more than 50 cities were doing so, and by 1990, more than 60 percent of all cities with populations of more than 100,000 had established neighborhood associations.

While we do not have more recent comprehensive data, several developments are noteworthy. Some cities, including large ones such as Los Angeles, have created new systems of neighborhood representation over the past decade. And other municipalities with established systems have continued to innovate, substantially increasing their capacity and developing new forms of partnership with a broad range of other neighborhood, civic, business, and environmental groups.

Citywide systems of neighborhood representation include all neighborhoods, not just those targeted for community development because of poverty or past discrimination. Neighborhood associations in these systems are nonpartisan by ordinance and cannot use their resources or communication media for partisan campaigns for mayor or city council. They have extensive two-way communication channels with city hall and multiple ways to exercise voice, though they tend to be most effective on local land-use issues and least effective on citywide issues such as mass transit, downtown development, and school reform. Neighborhood associations may have staff paid by the city, but many also raise other funds as incorporated nonprofits with quasi-autonomous standing.

These neighborhood participation systems accommodate, complement, and encourage a wide range of other forms of citizen organizing and self-help. (See case profile of Seattle's neighborhood matching fund.) Independent groups more often initiate action, but neighborhood associations play a strong role in the outcome. Neighborhood associations work with groups such as the Sierra Club, Audubon Society, and other local environmental groups, senior and youth organizations, as well as local chapters of the League of Women Voters and United Way. Often the associations collaborate with CDCs, sometimes having played a key role in establishing them. In citywide systems, neighborhood associations neither co-opt nor supplant various independent forms of citizen action and they generate increased trust within neighborhoods and between neighborhoods and city government. They also tend to lower the participation inequalities between different income and racial groups.

Portland, Oregon, illustrates some of the dynamic potential of a well-designed system of neighborhood representation. The Office of Neighborhood Associations was created in the early 1970s in response to citizen organizing and federal programs such as Community Action and Model Cities. In the 1990s, it was restructured as the Office of Neighborhood Involvement to become more inclusive of other kinds of civic organizations, more responsive to lower-income communities, and more capable of facilitating leadership development, problem solving, and dispute resolution. In addition, a community planning office facilitates citizen deliberation to develop workable plans within an antisprawl framework and recruits former neighborhood activists to staff it. "Neighborhood district attorneys" throughout Portland work not as litigators but as problem solvers with neighborhood groups, and community police officers partner with citizen efforts. Multistakeholder partnerships work for comprehensive community revitalization in minority and poor neighborhoods, such as Albina, where 41 different civic and nonprofit groups and an equal number of government agencies, schools, universities, and business groups were involved in implementing the plan developed through 140 public meetings over a 3-year period.

In Portland, watershed councils also operate as multistake-holder partnerships for ecosystem restoration. The Johnson Creek Watershed Council, for instance, has engaged more than 175 civic, government, and school groups plus 8,000 citizens in hands-on restoration efforts. Schools, colleges, and youth groups partner with the city's bureau of environmental services to prevent storm water runoff and to train watershed stewards. Portland State University (see below) has also restructured its curriculum to provide extensive opportunities for community-based learning in which students work directly with neighborhood and environmental groups and community agencies.

Traditional civic groups in Portland have declined over the past generation, much in line with the findings of some national studies on the decline of social capital. Yet these traditional groups have been replaced by an even larger panoply of more inclusive and dynamic advocacy groups and collaborative partnerships capable of grappling with increasingly complex problems on a sustainable basis. The system of neighborhood associations has been an essential component of this process.

Neighborhoods USA is the main national network that facilitates an exchange of best practices of participatory neighborhood governance and self-help. Its annual conferences bring together 1,000 or so neighborhood activists, association leaders, and staff members of city departments of neighborhoods and typically include a wide array of civic organizing approaches: assets-based community development, faith-based organizing, environmental justice, healthy communities, parish nursing, and sustainable development. Professional associations, such as the American Planning Association, International City/County Management Association, and National League of Cities have also increasingly promoted participatory models of governance, self-help, and planning in recent years. The Project for Public Spaces works with local groups, as well as city and state planning and transportation agencies, to help design spaces that promote vital community life and civic interaction.

City of Seattle's Neighborhood Matching Fund

In addition to facilitating extensive citizen participation in developing neighborhood plans to meet Seattle's commitment to the state's growth management act, the Department of Neighborhoods provides matching grants on a competitive basis for neighborhood improvement, organizing, and planning projects. Local groups must match the dollar value of the grant with donated materials, cash, and/or labor (at $12 per hour for unskilled labor and market value for skilled services). Most are "small and simple" grants of less than $15,000, but larger grants can run as high as $100,000 and in some cases even more. Neighborhood associations, watershed groups, ethnic associations, PTAs, youth groups, gay and lesbian groups, historical preservation societies—any democratically governed neighborhood group—can qualify. The city neighborhood council, composed of 13 district council representatives, judges the applications. Its criteria include self-help, diversity, citizen participation, environmental sustainability, and collaboration.

Matching grants, amounting to $4.5 million for some 418 projects in 2001, enables community groups to build and renovate playgrounds, restore streams and forests, plant community gardens, design public art, and implement any number of other collaborative neighborhood self-help projects. For instance, one group designed a beautiful "salmon slide" as part of a trail for kids that teaches them about the salmon's upstream migration. The slide is linked to a creek restoration project designed and implemented by another group. A separate fund encourages participation of neighbors with developmental disabilities in creek restoration and other projects, and a new pilot fund encourages race relations and social justice projects with community-building goals. Each year, the department hosts an Ideas Fair, as well as workshops and tours of ongoing and completed projects, so that citizens with model projects and innovations can provide peer assistance to other neighborhoods. More than 2,000 projects have been completed to date.

The department also facilitates the development of new neighborhood associations and outreach to enable established organizations to become more inclusive. It provides ongoing workshops in leadership development, organizing, and volunteering. Tens of thousands of individuals have become involved through the matching fund, some for the first time. The department's Web site features descriptions of all matching grant projects, as well as all neighborhood plans and progress reports on their implementation, thus adding further transparency to an already open and democratic process of planning.

Community Visioning, Study Circles, and Deliberative Dialogues

Other approaches to community problem solving and community development have burgeoned in recent years as well. Several of the more important ones are community visioning, study circles, and public issues forums, plus other significant variants based on deliberative dialogue among citizens.

Community visioning engages citizens in articulating a broad vision of what they would like their city or region to look like in the future and then uses their civic energy to develop various projects and partnerships to realize that vision. This often begins with a dozen or so "champions" of the process, drawn from a diverse set of organizations and demographic groups, who then broaden the range of stakeholders to perhaps 60–80 through one-on-one recruitment, focus groups, town meetings, and other highly visible public events.

Diversity of stakeholders at the table is key to success, as representatives of the old guard join with innovators and groups previously excluded from power and planning. A committee often provides research support on current trends, community perceptions, and likely paths of development in the absence of a new vision and strategy. It may also oversee an assessment of the community's civic infrastructure through the National Civic League's *Civic Index.* With an ethos of openness to all in the community, another committee develops broad outreach, often by engaging civic and professional associations in new ways and around a renewed commitment to the common good. A neutral, outside facilitator oversees the overall process, even as stakeholders provide leadership and facilitation for many of its components. Indeed, visioning is designed to generate a plethora of ideas from ordinary citizens, develop leadership skills for future collaboration, and build trust across boundaries.

Elected officials sometimes serve as the initial advocates of visioning. A growing number of "facilitative leaders" have been elected to office; they believe that a critical part of their job is to convene citizens and stakeholder groups in dialogues that tackle tough issues. Increasing numbers of agency staff are also becoming skilled in visioning methodologies. However, public officials generally do not drive the process, but remain "the caboose on the civic train."

Inspired by the success of visioning in communities such as Chattanooga, Tennessee, (see case profile) many communities have engaged in communitywide visioning. As *Governing Magazine* noted a few years ago, "A highly contagious bug ... has been sweeping civic America in the late 1990s: visioning fever." Even when many projects stall or proceed initially in top-down fashion, citizens often persist in broadening representation and shifting to concrete action. Indeed, as one scholar has noted, "'visioning' is a euphemism for participation and power" that raises the question of whether ordinary citizens define and take ownership of the future of their communities.

Study circles are small, diverse groups of 8-12 participants who convene regularly over a period of weeks or months to address a critical public issue. They use trained, impartial facilitators recruited from the community, along with nonpartisan discussion materials. These circles meet in neighborhoods and across cities, counties, regions, and school districts. A study circle process might involve hundreds, even thousands, of people convening during the same period with the aim of sharing personal experiences with an issue, discussing the many points of view in the community, and considering strategies for action. While the process does not require consensus, it does aim to uncover areas of agreement and common concern. Ideally, the process is driven by a set of local leaders or organizations that represent the diversity of the community. The process attempts to build on and complement other innovative civic efforts at community-building, visioning, service learning, civic journalism, and collaborative problem solving and to generate new sources of trust and relationships through face-to-face deliberation.

Over the past decade, hundreds of communities have engaged in communitywide study circle programs on a broad array of issues: race and race relations, crime and violence, growth and sprawl, youth and families, school reform, and police-community relations. Some communities have used study circles as a core component in developing a wide variety of community-building activities. On the southwest side of Delray Beach, Florida, for instance, study circles built on prior community organizing against drug abuse and then moved to establish an innovative Village Academy school that combined K–12 education with a broad range of social, civic, and vocational opportunities. Participants then developed a new structure for neighborhood associations and engaged in community visioning for the city's Vision 2010 initiative. In Portsmouth, New Hampshire, circles began as Days of Dialogue: Respectful Schools, in which 200 sixth graders in a middle school met with 75 community and school board leaders, parents, and business people to talk about bullying and other student behavioral issues. The trust that emerged led to another round of study circle dialogue and to collaborative action on the highly charged issue of school redistricting, which had been stalemated in polarized city council meetings. Study circles have now also become part of developing Portsmouth's ten-year master plan.

Public issues forums have much in common with study circles but also use "issue books" with a range of alternative frames to guide citizen deliberation and cover numerous public issues beyond local community development. *Deliberative polling* uses a random sampling to simulate community, state, and national deliberation on a single issue or set of issues among an assembled group of citizens. The range of other models for citizen deliberation on public issues includes *citizen juries* and *consensus councils.*

The 21st Century Town Meeting™ combines small group dialogue, networked computers, electronic keypads, and large video screens to enable large groups of citizens, as well as organized stakeholders, to develop compelling recommendations on public policy in a time frame that aligns with a modern cycle of governance and media coverage. Listening to the City, for instance, assembled more than 4,300 people in July 2002 to deliberate over plans for the reconstruction of Ground Zero in the wake of 9/11 and made recommendations that public officials then directed designers to include as they returned to the drawing boards. The deliberations themselves grew out of ongoing work by the Civic Alliance to Rebuild Downtown New York, a coalition of more than 85 business, labor, civic, and community groups committed to vigorous public discussion. The coalition then formed a partnership with the Lower Manhattan Development Corporation and the Port Authority of New York and New Jersey, which share formal authority for the site. Unfortunately, these two organizations did not effectively follow up on this promising start and the civic sector alone could not sustain the momentum.

Various organizations have been central to the development and diffusion of these various models of civic deliberation. The Study Circles Resource Center (SCRC) has worked directly with several hundred communities; many others use its published materials. Martha McCoy, director of SCRC, has also been active in linking study circles to a broad range of civic renewal movement networks. The National Issues Forums Institute and the Kettering Foundation have collaborated to develop nonpartisan issue books. More than 22 regional public policy institutes have been established to promote forums among hundreds of thousands of citizens in a broad array of groups: youth organizations, university extension programs, women's groups, senior citizen programs, libraries, literacy programs, schools, civic and environmental groups, neighborhood associations, correctional facilities, colleges, and universities. The National Civic League (NCL) has played an important role in community visioning work through its consulting and publishing. A much broader network of local innovators has also used NCL's *Civic Index* to evaluate their capacities and practices to chart new approaches. NCL's All-America City Awards provide an especially important focus for catalyzing and evaluating this work among more than 100 communities each year.

The Pew Partnership for Civic Change has worked with several dozen small- and medium-sized cities, using a variety of these and other methodologies. America*Speaks* has used the 21st Century Town Meeting™ for city-resource allocation, regional planning, and national policy formation, as well as for the 4-H National Conversation on Youth Development (see below).

During the 1996 presidential campaign, the National Issues Convention (NIC) assembled 459 citizens for several days in Austin, Texas, and was covered widely on national media. The NIC brought heightened visibility to deliberative polling, now promoted in a variety of state and local venues through the Center for Deliberative Polling. In early 2003, another convention met in Philadelphia to deliberate about "American's Role in the World."

While there are no reliable statistics on overall growth, several organizations show an increase in numbers of communities and organizations using various visioning and deliberative democratic methodologies over the past decade. Some speak of a "deliberative democracy movement." The National Coalition on Dialogue and Deliberation, now working in partnership with the Deliberative Democracy Consortium, was founded in the wake of a national conference in 2002 that included many of these and other groups of dialogue practitioners and demonstrated a rich variety of practices as well as overlap among them.

On a related front, the National Association for Community Mediation represents a blossoming "community mediation move-ment" that sees itself engaged in collaborative problem solving "in the tradition of democratic self-governance." Local centers typically employ a few staff members and train dozens of volun-teer mediators, focusing on a broad range of disputes and often complementing the work of other neighborhood organizations or community policing efforts. Over the past decade, these centers have grown from approximately 150 to more than 550, in some cases receiving significant state support. One estimate places the number of citizens trained in community dispute resolution at 76,000 and the number of active volunteer mediators at 19,500. The Association for Conflict Resolution represents some 6,000 professional practitioners, many of whom also provide critical resources for community problem solving and civic innovation.

Communitywide Visioning in Chattanooga

"What are your goals, hopes, and dreams for Chattanooga? "This was the question posed in 1984 to nearly 2,000 citizens engaged in a 20-week series of visioning sessions known as Vision 2000. The common vision they generated of a city abandoning its polluted past and becoming a model of sustainable development brought in environmental groups, neighborhood associations, business leaders, academic institutions, public agencies, and elected officials. Out of this first phase emerged 223 projects and a number of new organizations dealing with neighborhood revitalization and sustainable development. A decade later, ReVision 2000 engaged another 2,600 citizens and produced more than 100 specific recommendations in a process designed both to generate collaborative action and create a political mandate for change.

These visioning processes, led by the nonprofit Chattanooga Venture, included a board of some 50 leaders from a diverse range of organizations and constituencies and trained some 200 citizens to facilitate public meetings among neighborhood groups, civic organizations, and professional associations. Civic sector leaders, such as the Lyndhurst Foundation, were joined by business leaders in the Chamber of Commerce who were willing to confront issues of pollution and sprawl. Several city councilors with activist backgrounds lent their support, as did the mayor, who helped ensure that public bureaucracies would be responsive to new collaborative ventures such as that between the Department of Parks and Recreation and the Trust for Public Lands. The Tennessee Valley Authority worked with environmental groups and schools and helped bring about downtown revitalization and the start-up of a new fleet of electric buses.

The Chattanooga Greenways program, through a partnership of the Trust for Public Land and local neighborhood associations, has created a 75-mile network of protected corridors of open space linking many parks and recreation areas. RiverValley Partners, now part of the Chamber of Commerce, has spurred various sustainable development initiatives, including the Aquarium and Tennessee Riverpark. The regional planning agency also continues to involve thousands of citizens in the "Futurescape Community Planning Process."

While the visioning process has generally been based on civic collaboration, it was preceded by a decade of grassroots environmental action. And it provided the opportunity for low-income and minority groups to confront other stakeholders to ensure that their own issues, such as affordable housing and environmental justice, would also become part of the broad agenda.

Community Policing, Youth Courts, and Community Justice

Community policing has become an important paradigm over the past decade, challenging some core tenets of the dominant professional, top-down model of policing ascendant through much of the twentieth century. This model, based on classic tenets of "scientific management," relied especially on rapid response by cruising officers typically removed from the life and everyday networks of the community. New initiatives among a nationwide network of police managers, policy intellectuals, and federal agencies, along with widespread support in communities, has led to the development of a community policing movement, which some see as part of a larger community justice movement encompassing many other aspects of public safety and criminal justice.

Community policing articulates four broad principles. First, organizational decentralization sheds layers of bureaucracy to enable officers to communicate more effectively with citizens, build trust at the street level, and develop local solutions for local problems. Second, rather than simply responding to discrete crime incidents, officers develop broad, proactive problem-oriented strategies that focus on patterns and causes of crime. This often requires collaboration with other city and human service agencies (for example, to remove abandoned vehicles, provide lighting for streets, alter public transportation routes, enforce housing codes, or help locate job and youth programs). Third, the community is involved in defining and analyzing the problems, and its concerns with fear-inducing *conditions* (such as physical decay and social disorder), rather than just lawbreaking *incidents*, are taken seriously by officers. Fourth, citizens are viewed as important "coproducers" of public safety, working with police to solve problems and eliminate conditions that could lead to more serious crime. The theme of police agencies working "collaboratively" and in "partnership" with a range of community-based organizations has now become the centerpiece of many department mission and vision statements.

Thus, citizens organize neighborhood crime watches, many of which have developed sophisticated surveillance and problem-solving capacities. Local residents repopulate streets through "positive loitering," organize escort services for the elderly, and create "safe school zones." To ensure safety for women and girls, many march to "take back the night" as a form of symbolic and practical civic ownership. Citizens also enlist the power of religion in their battles to control public space by holding prayer vigils in the midst of street drug markets to drive them out of the neighborhood. In addition, local residents clean up graffiti and gang taggings and picket the homes of landlords whose buildings are sites of crime and violence—even encouraging them to get "landlord training" so they can become competent coproducers of public safety as well. Residents develop education programs to help neighbors secure their homes and report crime rapidly to the police. They volunteer in mediation and cooperative truancy reduction programs with schools. In some cases, citizens even help redesign the physical properties of the neighborhood to encourage more vibrant civic interaction.

Cities have varied in the design of community policing programs. Some limit these programs to a designated group of officers, often volunteers, while others involve all regular patrol officers. Some cities make very limited efforts to involve citizens, while others build on previous citizen-organizing around crime and community development. In Chicago, community policing reforms have combined extensive training of officers and ambitious efforts at interagency coordination with systematic citizen participation through beat meetings and district advisory committees (see case profile).

Youth courts (or teen courts) represent another dimension of community justice. These courts engage youth as jurors and sometimes as judges, prosecuting attorneys, defense attorneys, bailiffs, and other court officers. They typically hear cases of first-time offenders, 14–16 years of age, in crimes such as shoplifting, vandalism, minor assault, disorderly conduct, and drug and alcohol use. While some youth courts engage in fact finding and adjudicate guilt or innocence, most focus on developing appropriate sentences that can help repair the damage done to victims and the larger community. Such sentences can include community service, restitution, formal apologies to victims, and subsequent service on teen juries for the purpose of active civic learning, responsibility, and empowerment. The principles of "restorative justice," increasingly used in youth courts, enhance their community-building and community problem-solving potential. Most youth courts are based in the juvenile justice system or in a community setting, though some also operate through schools and have built relationships with peer mediation programs.

The youth court movement has grown substantially over the last decade. In 1991, there existed only 50 youth courts in 14 states. By 2000, some 650 such courts had been established, and as of November 2004, there were 943 in 48 states and the District of Columbia. With an estimated 100,000 cases per year, youth courts are becoming a major component of the juvenile justice system (which handles some 750,000 cases annually in which no formal charges are filed). Youth courts enjoy substantial support in communities and are established through the efforts of many organizations and agencies, including the Junior League, YMCA, American Legion Auxiliary, bar association, sheriff's office, and police department. State governments have also begun to provide support. National organizations (such as the American Parole and Probation Association, American Bar Association, Street Law, Constitutional Rights Foundation, Phi Alpha Delta Public Service Center) and federal agencies (such as the Office of Juvenile Justice and Delinquency Prevention and the National Highway Traffic Safety Administration) have also provided key support for local programs, as well as for the work of the National Youth Court Center, the key movement network.

The community justice movement encompasses still other innovations in "community sanctioning," "restorative justice," "community courts," "problem-solving courts," and informal dispute resolution. Cities such as Portland, Oregon, have intro- duced neighborhood district attorneys as part of "community prosecution." Their key role involves working with citizens and police to bring diverse parties to the table in order to develop consensus and forge solutions to problems, especially low-level disorder crime and negative street behavior. Cook County (Chicago) also has created a community prosecutions division that works with the community through beat meetings and district advisory committees, primarily seeking civil remedies and using public education strategies.

Chicago Alternative Policing Strategy (CAPS)

In the early 1990s, as crime increased, city budgets stretched, and communities mobilized to protest heavy-handed police tactics, especially in minority communities, Mayor Richard Daley opted for an experiment in community policing that has since become institutionalized across the city. The CAPS program involves the entire department, not just special units, and has reorganized assignments around 279 beats of roughly 10,000 residents each, grouped into 25 districts. The reform envisions problem-solving systems with police coordinating their work with other city agencies and collaborating with citizens and community organizations through beat meetings and district advisory committees.

Training has been extensive for officers and sergeants, as well as for civilian beat activists and facilitators. During one two-year period, for instance, the Chicago Alliance for Neighborhood Safety dispatched teams of community organizers, civilian trainers, and experienced police officers to each city beat and trained some 12,000 residents. Some 7,500 police officers were also trained.

Beat meetings are monthly gatherings of citizens and police officers assigned to the local beat. Two dozen people from the neighborhood typically attend, along with five to seven officers. Ideally, they collaborate in identifying problems, as well as solutions, although about one-third of the meetings find police in the lead role and another third have citizens and existing community organizations as independent operators. Only a small percentage, however, pursue adversarial strategies. Citizens also often identify self-help strategies.

In the first year-and-a-half of the reform, approximately 15,000 beat meetings occurred; participation has remained substantial since then as a result of aggressive marketing and outreach. Approximately 6,000 Chicagoans attend monthly. Participation is highest in African American communities (where many meetings are held in churches), in high poverty areas, and in those neighborhoods with higher rates of violent crime, although homeowners and more-educated residents attend in disproportionate numbers. Citizens who attend beat meetings find them generally quite productive in addressing neighborhood problems, and African Americans report the greatest improvements. At the district level, commanders and civilian chairpersons have assembled advisory committees of diverse community leaders from civic, business, and professional organizations, along with ex officio agency representatives, to set broad strategies in fighting crime, as well as contributing to overall community development.

Civic Environmentalism

"Civic environmentalism" emerged as a distinct paradigm in the 1990s, though innovations were underway at least a decade earlier. Civic environmentalists generally support federal regulation and recognize the substantial gains in controlling point-source pollution since the 1960s. Yet they argue that command-and-control regulation, pollutant by pollutant, often proves inadequate in the face of the increasing complexity of problems, multiple sources of nonpoint pollution, and threats to entire ecosystems. Regulation needs to become more creative and more catalytic of collaborative, place-based problem solving that engages a broad range of citizens, institutions, and organized stakeholders, including traditional adversaries, in a process of continuous, mutual learning and adaptive management. The holistic and integrated science of ecosystems requires far richer civic approaches than those typically found in the polarized interest group competition, which too often results in policy stalemate.

Innovative civic models and self-identified movements have emerged in many environmental policy arenas. These include the "watershed movement," "community forestry movement," "ecosystem restoration movement," "grassroots ecosystem management movement," "sustainable communities/sustainable cities movement," "environmental justice movement," and "land trust movement"—some of which, of course, overlap each other.

Watershed Movement

The watershed movement encompasses a wide array of citizen groups and support organizations at every level of the federal system. At the grassroots level are groups that call themselves "watershed associations" and "watershed alliances," "friends of the river" and "adopt-a-stream" groups, "save the bay" and "estuary alliances," "water monitoring partnerships," "stewards," and many other designations indicating civic vigilance and active restoration. Such groups are joined by many other civic associations, such as scout troops, senior volunteer groups, neighborhood and homeowner associations, sporting clubs (including kayakers, hikers, anglers, and boaters), religious congregations, and chapters of the League of Women Voters. Water-quality monitoring and hands-on restoration are central activities in many school science classes and service-learning projects. University centers also support watershed strategies and partner with civic associations.

A broad range of local, state, and federal agencies and interagency partnerships have come to support a robust role for citizen monitoring and restoration as part of a distinct "watershed approach," now firmly established in policy and administration. What increasingly unites these various groups is a belief that citizen vigilance is necessary to stop the further degradation of watersheds and that the complexity of watershed ecosystems requires many sources of local intelligence and civic initiative, in partnership with regulatory and business organizations, to restore them.

Thus, for example, the National Estuaries Program, administered by the U.S. Environmental Protection Agency (EPA), was established in 1987 with a core mission of enabling local estuarine constituencies to organize themselves and cooperate in developing long-term conservation plans. The Estuary Restoration Act of 2000 requires the Army Corps of Engineers to provide funding to help build local civic capacity and work collaboratively with community groups in restoration projects. The Chesapeake Bay Program (see case profile), also administered by the EPA, enables civic partnership strategies across a 64,000 square-mile drainage area, with some 150 rivers and streams contributing to the bay's freshwater flow.

At the state level, the watershed movement is manifest in an increasingly well-developed set of strategies to support ecosystem restoration in partnership with civic, government, university, and business groups. In Massachusetts, for instance, two dozen watershed associations on the major rivers came together in 1991 to form the Massachusetts Watershed Coalition. They developed a partnership with the state's executive office of environmental affairs, headed by a kindred civic innovator from Save The Bay in Rhode Island, to launch a watershed initiative built on civic environmental principles. As of the late 1990s, there were approximately 30 watershed associations and councils on the major rivers, 40 more subwatershed alliances and "friends" groups, 70 collaborative civic and agency "stream teams" and monitoring groups, and a total of perhaps 1,000 other grassroots groups of various sorts, including land trusts and conservation commissions, exercising some form of citizen stewardship over the state's watersheds.

The Rivers Council of Washington, with networks to several hundred watershed associations and kindred groups and a mission to "reinvent the environmental movement from the ground up," works with the Department of Ecology and other agencies to develop "holistic, community-based, and consensus-building strategies." The Oregon Watershed Enhancement Board provides substantial funding for multistakeholder watershed councils committed to citizen involvement in the development of watershed action plans and voluntary restoration work.

Watershed groups, of course, vary widely. Often they start out as advocacy groups in contention with a private developer or government agency and, if they survive their initial battles and gain a respected seat at the table, slowly come to appreciate the need for long-term collaborative projects. Alternatively, they may start out as small stewardship and restoration projects and gradually become part of larger networks along an entire river or watershed. Some multistakeholder partnerships, such as the Henry's Fork Watershed Council in Idaho, form only after years of adversarial conflict and stalemate. Others, such as the Mattole Restoration Council in California, begin by drawing in a broad array of community service groups, land trusts, fishing associations, and worker co-ops to do hands-on restoration work and then broaden to more difficult and contentious issues with ranchers and loggers. Save The Bay in Rhode Island not only advocates at the state house and opposes environmentally destructive development, but it also engages a wide variety of local civic, boating, and school groups in monitoring the Narragansett Bay and restoring it through hands-on work. Still others, such as the Long Island Sound Watershed Alliance, bring together several hundred groups.

Estimating the overall number of groups in the watershed movement is a tricky business, though it seems clear that the past decade has witnessed manifold growth. *The 2003 River and Watershed Conservation Directory*, developed jointly as part of a movement-building strategy by the River Network and the National Park Service's Rivers, Trails, and Conservation Assistance program, lists some 3,600 grassroots river and watershed conservation groups, national nonprofits, and government agencies but recognizes this number as a considerable underestimate. It does not, for instance, inventory the hundreds of local chapters of national environmental organizations that work on river and watershed issues nor the thousands of youth and school groups. The directory does not include thousands of groups listed in independently developed local partnership directories or state directories, such as the University of California at Davis inventory, which counted 660 watershed groups in the state in the late 1990s. Nor does it include the hundreds, if not thousands, of local conservation commissions for whom watershed protection is a central concern.

Another reputable estimate of a much narrower subset of "grassroots ecosystem management" (GREM) projects in the West engaged in collaborative governance among previously contentious stakeholders puts them in some 500 communities, with an estimated 40,000 core participants and volunteers. The GREM model engages citizens as members of *both* interest groups (such as farmers and environmentalists) *and* communities. It builds an integrated community-based network to nurture trust, deliberation, and collaboration in the framework of a commonly defined community history and identity. GREM combines a formal institutional structure that is participatory and nonhierarchical with informal decision-making institutions that can improve overall governance and accountability through a focus on results measured by mutually defined sustainability indicators. Edward Weber calls this "simultaneous, broad-based accountability" to the major stakeholders, as well as to the public agencies responsible for natural resources and land management. GREM partners mobilize community assets and ordinary citizens' knowledge in collaboration with professionals and seek to align profit motives and opportunities with ecological sustainability. In fact, the idea of community assets, formulated initially in the community development field, has now become a key concept in sustainability science.

At the national level, the River Network works with 700 partners, including statewide groups such as the Rivers Council of Washington and the Massachusetts Watershed Council, in training, organizational development, and coalition building. In the late 1990s, the River Network convened the "watershed innovators workshops" in different regions of the country. The workshops helped establish the identity of the "watershed movement" and a vision of "watershed democracy." The River Watch Network (now part of the River Network) has trained 16,000 volunteer monitors and assisted more than 800 school monitoring programs. Save America's Estuaries, a national coalition of 11 regional, coastal community-based organizations, such as Save The Bay and the Chesapeake Bay Foundation, has a combined membership of 250,000. It emphasizes community-based restoration in its national strategy and policy work, such as the passage of the Estuary Restoration Act of 2000. As a result of pressure from local member groups, national environmental organizations, such as the National Audubon Society, National Wildlife Federation, Sierra Club, and Izaak Walton League, have in recent years increasingly emphasized innovative civic strategies and partnerships.

Watershed approaches are central to environmental education through schools and youth organizations. The North American Association for Environmental Education has state affiliates in two-thirds of the states and an extensive network of individual environmental educators, many of whom use service learning to engage students actively in watershed monitoring and restoration. Earth Force has field offices in eight cities, from which it coordinates partnerships with middle schools for its Community Action and Problem Solving program and now oversees the Global Rivers Environmental Education Network, which has affiliated middle and high school groups and educators in every state and several other countries. Project WET (Water Education for Teachers) represents a network of teachers developing leadership, materials, and grassroots instruction, with programs in every state and the District of Columbia. The Student Conservation Association develops conservation leadership and community-building skills among a national network of teams of high school and college students, whom it places for extended periods of time with some 350 federal, state, and local agencies and environmental groups. The National Association of Service and Conservation Corps includes 106 corps in 37 states and the District of Columbia. The corps develop work and civic leadership skills among low-income young people through conservation and other service projects.

Chesapeake Bay Program

Initiated at a 1983 governors' summit that brought legislators from Maryland, Virginia, Pennsylvania, and the District of Columbia together, along with administrators, scientists, bay users, and environmental groups, the EPA's Chesapeake Bay Program sees a key part of its role as facilitating local civic action and capacity building for long-term restoration.

This program works with the states to develop new collaborative processes for land use planning, and its local government advisory committee provides technical assistance to local authorities to manage growth and form alliances with civic organizations. Its Participation Action Plan and Partnership Initiative are designed to support watershed associations, civic organizations, and land trusts in building the constituencies needed for effective governance. Its Partner Communities Program recognizes those that meet specific benchmarks for improvement. The Chesapeake Bay Program has also fostered "semiautonomous tributary teams" of scientists and government officials, agriculture and industry representatives, educators and realtors, and environmental and civic groups capable of authoring and implementing context-specific strategies through iterative learning linked to a broad conception of "citizen stewardship."

The Alliance for Chesapeake Bay coordinates the Citizens' Advisory Council of the program and provides educational and technical support for community projects within a nonadversarial framework. The Alliance's citizen monitoring program trains volunteers and facilitates the work of homeowner associations, service organizations, schools, and families that have formed stream teams and river watches to provide citizens and government with essential data on unusual discharges, trash dumps, fish kills, algae blooms, and sewage leaks. The Alliance also administers the Chesapeake Bay Program's small grants that fund local restoration efforts and new watershed organizations. The Chesapeake Bay Trust serves as a general funder for many volunteer efforts and local partnerships. Since its founding in 1967, the Chesapeake Bay Foundation has provided critical advocacy and education.

Local conservation and restoration projects are proceeding in more than 1,000 communities, with the participation of a very broad array of civic organizations, sporting groups, businesses, and farmers' organizations. For instance, local efforts have sparked a general civic restoration strategy for oysters in the bay, where thousands of citizen "gardeners" nurture young oysters at home and school and then transplant them by hand to local reefs. While there is a long way to go before bay ecosystems are adequately restored and growth is managed effectively enough to sustain gains, widespread agreement exists among regulators and local stakeholders that civic strategies have been essential to the progress made to date and are vital to long-term success.

Land Trusts, Forest Planning, and Ecosystem Restoration

Land trusts that promote conservation have been around for decades. But as a former vice president of The Nature Conservancy (TNC) has noted, "In the 1980s, this modest, piecemeal cooperative effort exploded into a nationwide movement involving every major federal landowning agency, every state, [and] hundreds of localities." By 1990, there were 889 land trusts, and today there are more than 1,500 trusts, with more than 1 million local members protecting more than 9 million acres, a doubling since 1998, according to the most recent census by the Land Trust Alliance. These nonprofit organizations bring to land conservation a variety of advantages, such as networks of personal contacts with private landowners, volunteer land stewards to help maintain the land, and greater agility than government organizations have to purchase land and benefit from timely cost savings, In recent years, the larger state and national land conservation organizations have placed new emphasis on direct citizen involvement in restoring ecosystems. The Volunteer Stewardship Network (see case profile) established a model for the Illinois Nature Conservancy that has spread to other state conservancies, the national office of TNC, and the Audubon Society. TNC has also begun to stress facilitating partnerships with private landowners to maintain ecologically sustainable practices for working landscapes. In doing so, TNC recognizes that acquiring large tracts of land and then prohibiting most human activity on them has limits as a strategy and that the knowledge and moral sensibilities of traditional users must be mobilized in new ways to protect livelihoods and check the development of new subdivisions. This brings together traditional adversaries, such as environmentalists and ranchers, along with other community stakeholders, into self-described "community-building" partnerships. As one TNC program manager explained, "Our ultimate goal … is to support other stewards of the land on the land." In effect, it means enabling ranchers and farmers to work as "civic professionals" whose expertise is linked to building the civic capacity of the broader community to solve public problems.

Within the national forests, collaborative planning and stewardship became increasingly common during the 1990s in the wake of many fierce battles, and today there are hundreds of examples of success. The new paradigm is reinforced by a considerable body of theoretical work on common-pool resource management and ecosystem science. State, county, urban, and community forestry also include many forms of collaboration, and practitioners increasingly speak a language of relationship building, community visioning, and social capital that is virtually indistinguishable from urban community-building. The U.S.

Forest Service funded the training of several hundred thousand volunteers for urban and community forestry during the 1990s. Metropolitan "greenspace programs," such as the one in Portland, Oregon, (a model for many areas in the Northwest) might include as many as 60 FAUNA (Friends and Advocates of Urban Natural Areas) groups to serve as advocates and land stewards on an extensive network of collaboratively managed public and private land.

Over the past decade, leading innovators have been networking regionally and nationally through the Lead Partnership Group, Communities Committee of the Seventh American Forest Congress, National Network of Forest Practitioners, and National Community Forestry Center to shape a vision and share best practices for a "community forestry movement." The Lead Partnership Group's *Principles of Community-Based Forestry* includes a central place not only for multistakeholder partnerships and consensus decision making, but also recognizes a legitimate role for interest-based national groups that are often suspicious of place-based forms of collaboration. Its leaders are explicit about the movement's affinity with other civic environmental movements, as well as with other community-building movements that aim to revitalize democracy. They also link civic problem solving to strong norms of economic and environmental justice that can empower those who work the land, from loggers and woodworkers to disenfranchised poor and minority communities that depend on forest product gathering for their livelihoods.

Volunteer Stewardship Network

As a college student, Steve Packard had marched on Washington in 1963 to hear Martin Luther King, Jr. deliver his "I Have a Dream" speech. Then, in the 1970s, while working for a statewide environmental organization in Illinois, he gathered a group of volunteers to research the history of prairie and savanna ecosystems that had been nearly destroyed in metropolitan Chicago. Motivated by the beauty of wildflowers and a reverence for the land, these volunteers set out on a process of restoring ecosystems—work that they compared to the meticulous artistry of "building cathedrals." They cleared invasive species and debris, revived old Native American burn techniques, collected seeds, stored them in their garages, and grew them in their kitchens. By the early 1990s, some 5,000 citizens in the Volunteer Stewardship Network had labored on more than 200 sites and restored more than 30,000 acres around the state, many within Chicago and its immediate suburbs.

To do this work, the stewards learned to build relationships with thousands of homeowners, agency staff, preserve owners, animal rights activists, civic associations, businesses, and visitors to the restored sites. For Packard, this meant renewing the practice of democratic politics in the environmental movement and figuring out "how to do wholesome, ethical, effective environmental politics." In the process, the Volunteer Stewardship Network established a civic model now recognized by TNC nationally and emulated by a variety of state conservancies (within and outside TNC), which now see themselves as part of a larger "restoration movement," doing more than just buying up land to be managed by professional stewards.

Volunteer restoration work, however, has not come without its conundrums in Chicago and elsewhere, as some citizens have challenged what it means to "restore nature," questioned the science as well as the costs (to existing trees, wildlife, amenities, and public budgets), and even brought a temporary moratorium to projects in some areas. This has challenged the restoration movement to develop still broader understandings of citizen expertise and democratic process.

Today, the Illinois chapter of TNC supports the work of nearly 6,000 "citizen scientists," as TNC and the Audubon Society now refer to the stewards. Chicago Audubon also includes some 375 "frog monitors" among its network of citizen scientists. Chicago Wilderness, a partnership of more than 170 civic and environmental groups, institutions (such as zoos, museums, arboretums, and aquariums), and public agencies, which emerged out of these networks and now stretches across three states, has worked on 160 collaborative restoration projects since 1995. The Mighty Acorns program, for instance, engaged 8,000 urban fourth and fifth graders in restoring native environments. Chicago Wilderness has recently introduced assets-based community development principles into its urban work. The state of Illinois, also building on these models, now supports more than two dozen Ecosystem Partnerships as part of its Conservation 2000 (C2000) Ecosystems Program.

Environmental Justice Movement

The environmental justice (EJ) movement emerged from widespread, grassroots antitoxics campaigns in the 1980s. From its inception, it articulated a goal of "rebuilding democracy from community to community," with special focus on poor, working-class, and minority communities that had been largely shut out of both the environmental policy system and the mainstream environmental movement. The environmental justice movement gave voice to new community actors, especially women, who rose up in defense of homes, children, and neighborhoods. It asserted and won new rights, most importantly a "citizen's right to know," which has had a major impact on toxics policy and corporate practice.

While its often militant protest tactics, legal remedies, and "environmental racism" frame place the EJ movement squarely in the camp of social justice and rights organizing, local community groups have also stood in the forefront of many innovative civic strategies to reduce toxics and improve health. The right-to-know, for instance, has been operationalized in the Toxics

Release Inventory, one of the most successful environmental policies for reducing pollution, as well as for promoting collaborative problem solving among community groups and industry. Local community partnerships among churches, environmental groups, health departments, and local industry have developed communitywide strategies for monitoring and source reduction. Ethnic business associations, unions, trade associations, CDCs, statewide Head Start associations, urban gardeners' groups, historically black universities, and tribal colleges have collaborated on community education, green technology and process design, and broad strategies for community revitalization. Some corporations have also established community advisory panels with robust capacities for collaborative planning, problem solving, and citizen monitoring.

The major national environmental justice groups would not generally consider themselves part of a broad civic renewal movement and have often expressed strong criticism of those local groups that eventually pursue collaborative strategies. But the ethos at the grassroots, especially when environmental justice is part of broader community-development strategies and when environmental agencies provide needed funding and technical support, is to try to find ways to translate conflict into collaboration.

Environmental justice leaders working at the national level with the EPA also now speak of a major paradigm shift toward what they describe as the "environmental justice collaborative problem-solving model." The National Environmental Justice Advisory Council, established by the EPA with broad movement and other stakeholder and agency representation, has issued two recent reports that shift the original frame of the movement decisively by making community-based collaborative problem solving the centerpiece of pollution prevention strategies and cumulative risk assessment and reduction. This frame is also central to the new EPA Community Action for a Renewed Environment program. The shift to a collaborative EJ model has resulted not only from local organizing and the accumulation of science-based evidence on risk, but also from an EJ movement conversation with other civic models and movements, most notably assets-based community development, consensus building and dispute resolution, community visioning, healthy communities, and sustainable communities.

Dudley Street Neighborhood Initiative

In 1986, the Dudley Street Neighborhood Initiative (DSNI) in the Roxbury section of Boston waged its first organizing campaign around the theme "Don't Dump on Us." Since the Dudley Street area was home to innumerable legal and illegal trash dumps and transfer stations, as well as hazardous waste sites, DSNI began to incorporate a vision of environmental justice into its broader community development strategies for housing, jobs, and youth and family services in this multiracial, inner-city community.

While its organizing can be contentious, DSNI's core strategy is to build collaborative partnerships with local nonprofits, banks, businesses, government agencies, churches, and foundations. Its early battles with the city yielded DSNI eminent domain authority over 1,300 parcels of abandoned land that had been destroyed by arson, illegal dumping, or other forms of blight and contamination. To date, it has transformed 300 of these sites into high-quality affordable housing, community gardens, and other public spaces.

In its assets-based community development, DSNI has benefited from grants from the EPA's Office of Environmental Justice that are designed to build community capacity, as well as from a major EPA enforcement action that funded a "supplemental environmental project" (SEP). DSNI organized a grassroots campaign to promote environmental health. Its local gardeners' network has disseminated strategies to prevent lead poisoning, and youth from the community now work with suburban young people in The Food Project, in partnership with Massachusetts Audubon, to produce more than 200,000 pounds of organically grown produce annually for food pantries and inner-city farmers' markets.

With the SEP settlement, DSNI set out to develop a greenhouse (or bioshelter) on a contaminated brownfield site. The project has become part of a larger urban agriculture strategy. In 1996–1997, some 200 residents engaged in community visioning sessions to update and refine their visioning work of a decade earlier. An ambitious vision of urban agriculture emerged. This vision includes a community-supported farm, a network of community gardens, urban orchards, several bioshelters, food-processing facilities that market to restaurants, stores, farmers' markets, and directly through the Internet. Many now include these and related projects, such as The Food Project and Nuestras Raíces in Holyoke, Massachusetts, as part of an emerging "urban agriculture movement."

Engaged Campus

O n July 4, 1999, prominent leaders in higher education, including numerous university presidents, issued the *Presidents' Fourth of July Declaration on the Civic Responsibility of Higher Education*, affirming, "We have a fundamental task to renew our role as agents of democracy." Based on a decade or so of previous work in service learning and civic engagement at numerous colleges, a guide was provided for university leaders to assess progress at their own institutions. And they committed themselves to the task of helping to bring about and lead a national movement to renew the public purposes and civic mission of higher education. The *Declaration* was a fitting recommitment to the democratic ideals of the republic on Independence Day.

Civic Mission of Higher Education

The leaders of this movement argue that higher education has allowed its civic mission to erode in previous decades through overspecialization of disciplines oriented chiefly to self-referential professional associations and by permitting too many colleges to model themselves on elite research institutions. As a result, teaching has declined in importance, especially teaching that connects students and faculty to larger public purposes. With the triumph of positivism and formalism in many disciplines, research has become overly divorced from public problem solving, as well as from lay citizen and practitioner knowledge. Students, not surprisingly, have increasingly disengaged from politics. Even faculty offering critiques of injustice often find themselves reinforcing cynicism among students because their critiques have not been matched with genuine opportunities to build civic skills and effi-cacy. As we have become a more complex and diverse society that requires more continuous, interactive, and reciprocal strategies for "putting knowledge to work," we have let the core civic mission of our universities deteriorate.

The movement combines an expansive civic frame with a set of concrete practices of pedagogy, institutional engagement, and community partnership. Its leaders argue forthrightly that institutions of higher learning are vital agents and architects of a flourishing democracy, inextricably bound up with the reproduc-tion and renewal of its norms, practices, and traditions. Formal curricula can and should play an essential role in developing a range of civic competencies and habits, such as the arts of civil public argument, democratic deliberation, and critical analysis. Classroom and campus culture should model the norms of democratic respect and participation, especially those required for an increasingly diverse and complex democracy. Engagement in community service and action research can enhance student learning if structured carefully as part of curricula and can contribute to the production of public goods if done in genuine partnership with empowered community groups.

The university can also help form and re-form publics by acting as a convenor of diverse stakeholders to grapple with difficult and obdurate public problems. Rather than train students to become detached experts ready to impose technical solutions from above, the university can teach undergraduate, graduate, and professional school students the norms and practices of a "civic professionalism" that enables them to bring rich civic skills to their professional work.

The civic movement in higher education has an expansive democratic frame and large, transformative ambitions. At a strate-gy conference of academic innovators, community partners, and student leaders several years ago, Elizabeth Hollander, executive director of Campus Compact, urged, "Don't think small. The future of our democracy is at stake!"

Practices and Partnerships

Colleges and universities employ a wide variety of pedagogical practices, institutional change strategies, and forms of community partnership to enhance their civic mission. The most fundamental classroom pedagogy is service learning, also known as community-based learning, which links systematic study, research, and reflection to service off campus. Such service can be in community organizations, nonprofit social service agencies, social movement organizations, and public agencies, as well as in business and professional organizations committed to public and community goals. In some cases, service learning might also be tied to on-campus action projects, such as campus ecology, peace organizing, or campus diversity.

A recent study by a prominent team of researchers at the Carnegie Foundation for the Advancement of Teaching found three broad approaches in educating students as citizens: "community connections," "social justice," and "moral and civic virtue." The "community connections" approach is oriented toward building connections to particular communities and enhancing mutual problem-solving capacities. Thus, at Portland State University (see case profile), community-based learning places students in a wide range of neighborhood and watershed associations, as well as in family and child service agencies, community development corporations, planning departments, and advocacy groups. Spelman College, an historically African American women's college, defines its civic mission as developing dynamic leadership for two communities: the relatively poor, African American neighborhood near the college and the larger community of African Americans, especially African American women.

The "social justice" approach directly engages students and faculty in tackling systemic injustices. In many cases, this approach is rooted in the religious traditions of the college, such as the Catholic traditions of social justice at the University of Notre Dame and the College of St. Catherine. The latter also builds on the traditions of the Sisters of St. Joseph of Carondolet for the empowerment of women, which it incorporates into core requirements (a first-year course on the Reflective Woman), a senior capstone (the Global Search for Justice), and in programs designed to educate low-income women for careers in nursing, physical therapy, and other health-related fields. Some public universities, such as California State University at Monterey Bay, have also developed an explicit mission to foster social justice, with universitywide requirements on the analysis of power and equity, as well as democratic and community participation. The curriculum is anchored within a larger ethos of "ethical communication" designed to encourage pluralism and tolerance, rather than dogma, in how social justice is theorized and practiced in community-based learning and campus culture.

The "moral and civic virtue" approach stresses the inculcation of values, such as Chippewa tribal values and commitment to the common good at Turtle Mountain Community College in North Dakota. Civic virtues, however, can also be linked to service and action. Messiah College in rural Western Pennsylvania, founded by the Brethren of Christ, challenges students always to ask the question, "What would Jesus do?" Its interpretation of this question stresses the imperative to work for justice wherever injustice prevails and to combine this with good stewardship of economic and natural resources.

Needless to say, there is overlap in these approaches and also further opportunity for integrating and extending them. The University of Minnesota's Council on Public Engagement, for instance, stresses the possibilities of "public scholarship" in all disciplines, the civic dimensions of all professions, and the role of the university in catalyzing statewide public forums and problem solving. In President Robert Bruininks's view, every unit of the university should align itself with the mission of civic engagement. Scientists mapping the human genome have a special responsibility to engage the public on questions of ethics and public policy.

While much university civic engagement occurs through individual service-learning courses and collaborative action research projects, or through departments and professional schools, some institutions have developed substantial long-term institutional partnerships with communities. The University of Pennsylvania, for instance, has developed a comprehensive strategy for community development of the area of West Philadelphia, with a commitment of $200 million. This includes leveraging the university's contracting and hiring power to provide more jobs to the local community and to place a special emphasis on minority and women's businesses, as well as job training. This strategy also includes housing renovation for local residents and inducements for faculty and staff to move to the neighborhood to provide greater economic diversity and stabilization. It entails a major partnership with local schools to improve their educational performance and their capacity as hubs of civic problem solving. This West Philadelphia Improvement Corps is now a national model for university-school partnerships. These and other efforts draw in faculty and students through "problem-oriented teaching and research," for which there are now more than 100 courses. Many of these partnerships are coordinated through the Center for Community Partnerships. The center also works with a consortium of 42 colleges and universities in the area, the Philadelphia Higher Education Network for Neighborhood Development, to develop "mutually beneficial, sustained, and democratic community-based service-learning partnerships."

Although there are no comprehensive statistics that give an accurate picture of the extent of service learning and other civic engagement practices on campuses, it is clear that these have grown over the past decade as the movement has gained coherence. Campus Compact, the main institutional membership organization devoted exclusively to service learning and civic engagement (to which we shall return below), now counts nearly 950 member campuses nationwide—up from 300 in 1992 and 640 in 1999. Its annual membership surveys show a steady increase in the average number of faculty per campus offering service-learning courses. More institutions are also moving up the "service-learning pyramid" from introductory through intermediate to advanced levels of practice, as measured by a series of indicators. These include an explicit mission and purpose; administrative and academic leadership; external resource allocation to community partners; disciplinary, departmental, and interdisciplinary work; changed faculty roles and rewards; community voice in partnerships; and campuswide centers that enable such work.

Movement Networks

The civic movement in higher education has elicited support from numerous organizations, including the most prominent national trade associations. Collaboration among them has often been substantial. The American Association for Higher Education (AAHE) has played an important field-building role with its Engaged Campus for a Diverse Democracy project, multivolume series on Service Learning in the Disciplines, and national conference on the engaged scholar. It has collaborated with Campus Compact in establishing a national consulting corps to strengthen work on individual campuses. AAHE's widely read periodical, *Change: The Magazine of Higher Learning,* has also focused on engaged learning and the broader movement for civic renewal. The American Council on Education played an important early role in spurring collaboration on democratic engagement and cosponsored with Campus Compact the conference that produced the *Presidents' Declaration.*

Other associations have helped design strategies suitable for their member institutions. The Council of Independent Colleges has worked with dozens of its small liberal arts college members in disseminating service-learning practices and deepening institutional change strategies. To promote democratic skills and service learning for a "diverse democracy," the Association of American Colleges and Universities, the leading organizational voice on liberal education for all students, has developed extensive resources and training; in 2003, it established with Campus Compact a new Center for Liberal Education and Civic Engagement. The National Association of Independent Colleges and Universities has taken the lead in promoting student voter registration on college campuses and has been joined by Campus Compact, Youth Vote Coalition, and Project Vote Smart. Project Pericles represents a network of colleges and universities dedicated to institutional change involving all campus constituencies and the community to revitalize the democratic mission.

There have also been a number of important and sustained initiatives among public and land grant universities. The National Association of State Colleges and Land Grant Universities has promoted the idea of the "engaged campus" as a way to recapture the original mission of land grant universities. Many of its members have tailored the new mission to their own states, and national networks of university extension educators have taken up the challenge in their specific fields. The American Association of State Colleges and Universities has partnered with the *New York Times* on the "American Democracy Project" at 183 of its member campuses. Based on market research showing that students resonate much more with the university as a big window onto the world than as a narrow avenue for career advancement and competitive success, this project seeks institutional commitment to enhance intellectual and experiential understanding of civic engagement for undergraduates. In line with the 1988 "community-building" vision of the Commission on the Future of Community Colleges, the American Association of Community Colleges has helped develop service learning at dozens of institutions. In addition, the Community College National Center for Community Engagement provides a variety of resources for service learning and civic engagement.

Various other initiatives have been undertaken through professional, disciplinary, pedagogical, and other groups. The National Society for Experiential Education serves as an individual membership organization that includes college educators, as well as K–12, school-to-work, job training, and cooperative extension educators interested in service learning and other experience-based pedagogies. It has been holding annual national conferences since the early 1970s. The New England Resource Center for Higher Education has also worked with colleges and universities through its Civic Engagement Cluster and has done extensive professional development with faculty in this and related areas. An entire issue of *Academe,* published by the American Association of University Professors, has been devoted to the civic responsibility of higher education. The American College Personnel Association has created a civic education track at its national conventions. And the debate on civic renewal, public scholarship, and service learning has been taken up by a variety of disciplinary associations, such as the American Political Science Association and American Sociological Association ("public sociologies").

Other organizations focus on specific areas of collaborative work between communities and academia. Recognizing the centrality of the arts and humanities in democracy, Imagining America, a national consortium of colleges, universities, and cultural institutions, promotes the civic work of university artists, humanists, and designers working in partnership with communities. Community-Campus Partnerships for Health promotes genuine power-sharing and assets-mobilizing partnerships among communities and educational institutions to foster better health profession education, civic action, and healthy communities. It draws its membership from a broad array of academic institutions, health care organizations, and community groups, as well as government and foundations. Campus Ecology, a program of the National Wildlife Federation, fosters student leadership and broad stakeholder collaboration to develop and implement ecologically sustainable university practices.

Much of this practical work, of course, has been dependent on raising the big questions of democracy anew. The Kettering Foundation, especially through its *Higher Education Exchange* and national seminars on higher education and public life, has played an especially important role in catalyzing critical theoretical discussions on the role of the university in a democracy, as well as analysis of case studies and civic professional practice of teaching and scholarship. The Carnegie Foundation for the Advancement of Teaching has not only researched best practices, but has also challenged scholars to think deeply about democratic traditions and the role of the university in an information society. In 2002, the National Forum on Higher Education for the Public Good (formerly the Kellogg Forum) convened a series of national dialogues among more than 200 leaders to further commitment and public support for a multifaceted civic mission for higher education.

At the federal level, Learn and Serve, a program at the Corporation for National and Community Service, has supported extensive capacity-building projects among many of these national higher education organizations, as well as projects on individual campuses. Learn and Serve has also sponsored the National Service-Learning Clearinghouse as a general resource for higher education, as well as K–12 and community-based work. The Office of University Partnerships (OUP) at HUD, especially through its Community Outreach Partnership Centers program, has funded some 150 community-university partnerships engaged in community-building activities; many of these integrate service learning and student civic engagement as core components. OUP also sponsors and disseminates research to foster such work and helps link universities to extensive community development networks nationwide.

Campus Compact has been especially critical to the development of the civic movement in higher education. It is a professionally staffed, multitiered, and multistakeholder association with extensive networks of collaboration among other higher education organizations and within the broader civic renewal movement. Unlike the major trade and professional organizations, its sole focus is service learning and civic engagement in higher education. Campus Compact, founded in 1985, has grown to nearly 950 dues-paying institutional members (the bottom tier), 30 state compacts (the middle tier, which is growing steadily and provides substantial capacity for supporting local campuses), and a national office (the top tier) in Providence, Rhode Island, with a staff of 21. Campus Compact possesses substantial capacity for training and technical assistance, publicity, policy development, and documentation and dissemination of best practices. It coordinated the drafting of the *Presidents' Declaration on the Civic Responsibility of Higher Education,* widely disseminated as the core mission statement of the movement. It collaborates with virtually all major players in the higher education field who have shown interest in civic engagement and service learning, and it can enlist horizontal networks of practitioners for various projects. Under its leadership, a number of organizations have recently launched the Campaign for Civic Learning in College.

Founded by university presidents, who remain a core constituency, Campus Compact has developed multistakeholder representation and capacity among faculty, community service directors, and chief academic officers. Beginning with its Wingspread Summit on Youth Civic Engagement in March 2001, it has also begun to incorporate student representation much more directly into its operations, and its Raise Your Voice campaign has begun to extend this on a considerable scale.

The New Student Politics

The students who met at Wingspread articulated their alienation from traditional politics, as well as from forms of community service that seem little more than individual acts of charity. *The New Student Politics,* subsequently drafted by Sarah Long, a student at the summit, develops the idea of "service politics" as a relational politics of cocreation of public goods in which students are active producers of knowledge and democracy. This idea draws on some of their most robust experiences with service learning, as well as on the larger frame of the civic renewal movement. The Wingspread students do not reject politics; they recognize the need to engage traditional political institutions through voting, campaigns, protest, and policy development. Yet they seek to embed politics in relational public problem solving and community-building. The Wingspread students' "service politics" frame, in short, self-consciously aligns itself with much civic innovation outside the university.

In 2002, with *The New Student Politics* as a conceptual guide, Campus Compact launched Raise Your Voice, a national student campaign to increase civic and political engagement on campuses. The campaign began with another Wingspread summit in September, this time among leaders of many existing national student organizations. The steering committee for the summit included directors of the United States Student Association, Campus Opportunity Outreach League (COOL, now part of Idealist on Campus), and the Youth Vote Coalition. National service groups were represented by Habitat for Humanity (Campus Chapters and Youth Programs), Alpha Phi Omega, and Action Without Borders. Social justice and environmental groups included the NAACP (Youth and College Programs), Feminist Majority Leadership Alliance (Campus Outreach), National Student Campaign Against Hunger and Homelessness, National Youth Advocacy Coalition, Oxfam America, United Students Against Sweatshops, Global Justice (Student Global AIDS Campaign), Student Environmental Action Coalition, Campus Greens, and the National Council of La Raza (which also has a network of campus service groups). Among the other groups focused on voting were Rock the Vote and Votes for Students. College Democrats and College Republicans were also present.

While some of these organizations have well-developed professional staffs responsible for leadership training and campus outreach and can draw on the resources of a larger organization, others are looser and more decentralized. Together they represent as many as 6,000 local campus chapters and ad hoc groups.

While Raise Your Voice is still in its early stages, it represents considerable potential on a number of levels. First, it has provided the opportunity to build student leadership teams in those state compacts directly involved in the campaign, which begins to make students a full-fledged governing constituency alongside the other key stakeholders in the organization. Second, it has begun to develop networks that cut across the array of campus social justice, environmental, service, and voting groups active nationally and to raise the question of democracy as an integrative theme. And third, it has catalyzed some new activity and coordinated some existing activity in a way that can lead to genuine increases in student civic and political engagement. Each of these presents real challenges, to be sure. But the support of a professionally staffed, multitiered national association such as Campus Compact, which possesses substantial capacity for collaborating with a broad range of other professional and student organizations in higher education and with community partners and civic renewal organizations, promises to make the civic engagement of students today more sustainable than the participatory democracy of the 1960s student movements.

Portland State University

In the early 1990s, President Judith Ramaley and Provost Michael Reardon responded to a crisis of state funding and low retention rates at Portland State University in Oregon by revamping the curriculum in fundamental ways to suppor "community-based learning." The practice was hardly new at PSU, but it had existed in fragmentary form before the reform effort.

PSU is a predominantly commuter campus of 15,000 students with another 25,000 enrolled through the extension program. The development of the strategic plan for reform was a highly participatory process led by faculty with the collaboration of the community. Students, many of whom are adults with jobs and families, initiated the motto "Let Knowledge Serve the City." They now have extensive opportunities for community-based learning through their freshman inquiry courses, disciplinary majors, interdisciplinary programs, and senior capstones—a total of some 200 courses in all. The Center for Academic Excellence supports this work, evaluation is extensive and ongoing, and faculty rewards (including tenure and promotion) have been reconfigured to reflect the new emphasis.

Freshman inquiry courses are yearlong interdisciplinary courses required of all students. The Columbia Basin: Watershed of the Great Northwest, for instance, provides opportunities to integrate the study of economics, forest ecology, water resource management, native wildlife populations, Native American heritage, and local art and literature. This course provides citizen-students with the tools to build a holistic understanding that will enable them to engage actively in protection and restoration. Should a student continue in environmental studies, there are many other courses for active community-based learning.

For instance, Neighborhoods and Watersheds, a two-semester course with a capstone project, recently engaged student teams in a partnership with the Johnson Creek Watershed Council, Portland Watershed Stewardship Team, Portland Bureau of Environmental Services, and Friends of Zenger Farm. The last is an organic farm and wetland site that hopes to transform itself into an education and job-training center to teach and demonstrate sustainable techniques for building construction, wetland restoration, agriculture, and floodplain management. The students explore how to develop curricula that will serve various youth, job-training, and school-to-work programs. They also figure out how to build further partnerships with a local neighborhood association, local food coalition, and the association of general contractors in the interests of developing a shared vision for the farm.

In community-based learning at PSU, community groups and agencies are recognized as genuine co-teachers and are actively engaged in shaping the curriculum of many programs. The child and family studies program, for instance, was developed by faculty from 16 departments and offices on campus and 60 representatives of organizations and agencies that serve children and families in the metropolitan area. The institute of metropolitan studies has a board of representatives from communities across a five-county area.

Community Youth Development and K-12 Civic Education

While renewing the civic mission of higher education has become a self-conscious movement in the eyes of its leading practitioners and organizations, the broader field of youth civic engagement comprises several other distinct but related streams of innovation and public action that call themselves movements or are clearly on the path to doing so. Here we focus on two overlapping but distinct streams: 1) community youth development, which has added a strong emphasis on youth engagement to the youth development frame; and 2) civic education in K–12 schools, which embraces practices from classroom teaching about civics and government to innovative service-learning practices and youth empowerment in school governance. Both draw on the broader community service movement of the past two decades.

Community Youth Development

Around 1990, a number of prominent youth development scholars and practitioners began to develop a forthright critique of the dominant paradigm in their field. This paradigm viewed young people primarily as problems in need of "fixing" by outside professional and clinical intervention supported by separate silos of categorical funding (for substance abusers, runaways, and pregnant teens). It was becoming increasingly clear that such deficit-driven, crisis-oriented programs were very costly and had limited effectiveness. In addition, such programs bred an ethos of client dependence. Within a few years, the emerging frame of "positive youth development" began to include a central role for youth civic engagement in community development; many began to use the term "community youth development" (CYD) to denote this emphasis.

While not all practitioners and theorists share a common terminology, the new CYD frame includes, in varying combinations, the following components:

- *Assets* Shift from youth as problems to youth as problem solvers and resources.
- *Community* Young people do not grow up in programs; they grow up in communities. They can serve as agents of change creating sustainable and healthy communities.
- *Rights* Young people have basic rights to be seen, heard, and respected as citizens of the community and to be prepared as active participants in decision making that affects their lives.
- *Democracy* Young people are vital contributors to the everyday work of democracy today and need to learn the complex skills of democratic practice to serve a lifetime of effective engagement. Youth are vital coproducers of the democratic commonwealth. Without more robust engagement by young people, democracy in the United States is in jeopardy.
- *Partnership* Youth and adults can work in partnership— hence the increasingly common term "youth/adult partnerships"—and each needs to recognize the strengths and contributions that the other brings.
- *Pathways* Youth need multiple, visible pathways for developing civic skills and becoming change agents, and these pathways should extend across issues, types of organizations, and stages of the life course.
- *Inclusiveness* All youth, and not just youth-at-risk or high-achieving youth, should be the focus of youth engagement;

and this should occur in all settings, not just in separate youth projects or programs.

- *Work* Youth engagement involves real work of public value and genuine impact. It should not be confined to volunteering nor cut off from career interests. It is not just preparation for adult citizenship, but elicits real contributions today.
- *Learning* Active engagement constitutes a critical part of learning in school, work, and community activities; learning is cross-generational, active, and participatory.
- *Social justice* Youth engagement serves as a critical means to create more just communities and a just world.

CYD Movement Networks and Organizations

The CYD movement includes organizations ranging from some of the oldest national youth organizations in the country to small youth development agencies and organizing groups. Several nonprofit institutes and university centers have been especially important in developing components of the larger frame. Among these are the Forum for Youth Investment, whose conception of "youth action" maps diverse types and visible pathways of youth engagement. The Center for Youth and Communities at Brandeis University publishes the *CYD Journal,* which contains analytic tools, best practices, and case studies. It has also evaluated many national service-learning and civic engagement programs. The Center for Democracy and Citizenship at the University of Minnesota has thematized "democratic public work of real consequence" as central to robust youth engagement and has developed active citizenship curricula for wide dissemination in AmeriCorps and state extension programs, as well as through its own network of Public Achievement schools.

In addition, the Innovation Center for Community and Youth Development has been key to organizational capacity building, curriculum development, and research in large national organizations, such as the 4-H system (where it originated), as well as through the networks of diverse youth leadership and civic activism groups, such as those that have been part of the Youth Leadership for Development Initiative. Its work on youth/adult partnerships and youth in governance has been complemented by a greater focus on social justice in recent years. The Search Institute has been especially important in bringing the developmental assets framework to local coalitions in hundreds of communities. Youth on Board has provided leadership development to scores of national and local groups to institute effective youth governance and youth/adult partnerships. The Institute for Cultural Affairs has been a critical partner of various organizations, such as the National Network for Youth, in developing the CYD frame and providing training.

The Center for Youth Development and Policy Research at the Academy for Educational Development (AED) has provided important support for local and national organizations, including its collaborative project with the National Network for Youth and National 4-H Council on Transformational Community Development with Youth as Full Partners. The National Training Institute for Community and Youth Work at AED houses the National Building Exemplary Systems for Training Youth Workers (BEST) Initiative, which works through 15 core youth development agencies and several hundred local partners in 15 cities around the country to enhance professional development. Its Advancing Youth Development curriculum includes youth engagement as a central component.

Among the traditional multitiered national youth associations, National 4-H and the YMCA have each developed strategies to revive youth civic engagement as a core part of their mission and practice. To mark the centennial of the organization, 4-H leaders convened "local conversations" on the vision of youth development that involved some 40,000 youth and adults in 1,577 counties across the country during the fall of 2001. As an organization of 6.8 million youth from every county in the United States, these gatherings reflected the transformed demographics of 4-H, which over the years has become increasingly more urban and multiracial and includes significant numbers of children of migrant workers. Following the local conversations, another 8,000 people participated in state conversations and 1,200 individuals representing 400 organizations, including some from other national youth organizations, gathered at the centennial congress in 2002. As noted in its formal report, the "4-H movement" sees itself as part of the "youth development movement in America," dedicated to a common mission with central tenets of "empowering youth as equal partners" and "equal citizens." All communities need a "new generation of citizen leaders" and these must be developed by actively engaging youth on boards of nonprofits, local institutions, and government agencies. The report called for a "comprehensive civic education program through schools, community organizations, and private sector initiatives," with hands-on work and experiential learning as central components. These proposals have built on innovative service-learning and community problem-solving work among a network of 4-H leaders and clubs during the previous decade.

Likewise, during the 1990s, the YMCA of the USA has drawn on innovative programs such as Earth Service Corps and Young Adult Civic Connectors Initiative, as well as other service-learning and teen leadership programs. Its one hundred-fiftieth anniversary general assembly, in 2001, spoke of "reigniting the fire" of civic engagement. The following year it launched a national initiative that could learn from teams of practitioners from 40 innovative Y's around the country, as well as from the broad range of innovations in the civic renewal movement. (The latter was the topic of the first keynote address of the YMCA's inaugural symposium.) Some spoke of making the Y's "schools of democracy." The initiative has developed a network of "civic engagement fellows" across the system to promote the vision and help diffuse best practices and institutional culture change among local Y's themselves. In the first 18 months of the initiative, fellows provided more than 2,300 hours of workshop training to more than 14,000 adults and youth, including 7,694 local YMCA staff and volunteers. This represented a total investment of more than one million training hours.

The National Network for Youth, with a membership of some 800 local youth development organizations serving two million youth and families, has played a critical role in developing and diffusing the CYD approach since the early 1990s. Its annual symposia have provided important venues for showcasing civic engagement models of its member organizations (such as ROCA, El Puente, and Community Impact), as well as other national networks and local models. YouthBuild USA, the affiliated nonprofit network representing the majority of the 200 federally funded YouthBuild programs, has combined job training and community development with robust youth leadership development, from local job-site and classroom programming to neighborhood activism, media strategies, and congressional lobbying. The National Youth Court Center, as noted in our discussion of community justice, provides resources for the growing youth court movement.

An increasing number of cities have established youth commissions and councils to provide a formal youth voice in city government. Various models have been promoted through the National League of Cities and featured at national gatherings of organizations such as the YMCA of the USA and the National Network for Youth. In Hampton, Virginia, (see case profile) the youth commission of 24 students from the city's public and private high schools deliberates about a broad range of issues affecting young people, helps design problem-solving strategies, and works with youth planners on the city's comprehensive plan. But the commission is only one piece of a multifaceted strategy to build a civic engagement system and bring about deep "culture change" that includes active youth leadership development and voice in city agencies, neighborhoods, and the school system.

The San Francisco Youth Commission, composed of a very diverse group of 17 young people, emerged in 1995 out of a grassroots campaign by the city's "youth movement," as activists commonly refer to it. As part of the city's charter, the youth commission reviews all legislative and policy changes affecting young people. It also takes action on myriad issues ranging from leadership development for resisting sexual assault on girls and young women to school funding, public health education, and juvenile justice. Its work has triggered some important changes in the strategy of city agencies, such as the Department of Children, Youth, and Their Families and the San Francisco Unified School District, to actively involve youth in decision making. The Boston Mayor's Youth Council, created in 1994, is composed of 34 youths from the city's 16 major neighborhoods. Youth counselors develop relationships with adult staff and peer leaders at local youth agencies and community centers and advise the mayor and various agencies on policies and programs affecting young people. Boston's annual youth summits attract as many as 1,500 people.

Still other networks have been developing and refining various models of youth engagement. The "new girls movement" represents an increasing number of youth programs designed to empower girls and young women by creating safe spaces that are free of intimidation and by providing the leadership skills for them to become civically engaged in their communities. Many groups address the issues of sexism and violence against young women and girls, as well as the power of the media and popular culture to define body image in ways that can disable girls from becoming "authors of their own lives." Thus, for example, the

After-School Action Program/Girl World in Chicago provides 200 girls with leadership opportunities and links them to its larger network of tenant associations, congregations, and ethnic associations. Asian and Pacific Islanders for Reproductive Health, through its HOPE (Health, Opportunities, Problem-Solving and Empowerment) project, has trained dozens of young Cambodian women in action research and community organizing around the impact of sexual harassment on school achievement. The new girls movement has the support of the Ms. Foundation and 38 other foundations in the Collaborative Fund for Healthy Girls/Healthy Women, as well as networks of practitioners in the YWCA, Girls, Inc., Girl Power, and other organizations. While this movement draws from much feminist research and leadership development experience, it is also increasingly framing its work in terms of broad questions of democracy, civic engagement, and assets-based community youth development.

The community service movement has also been catalytic of civic engagement among youth. City Year, one of the key national networks that established an important model for other community service initiatives, has recently held high-level discussions among board and staff members on how its work might be seen as part of a larger "movement for democracy." The Grantmakers Forum on Community and National Service has transformed itself into Philanthropy for Active Civic Engagement in order to respond to increasingly diverse streams of civic activism coming into the movement. Public Allies develops young leaders (18–30 years old) for assets-based community development, and they in turn develop collaborative democratic leadership among local residents. AmeriCorps volunteers, in addition to their service in more than 2,000 nonprofits, faith-based organizations, and public agencies, have worked in numerous local, state, and national programs to build capacity for youth civic engagement and service learning, from the Boston College Urban Ecology

Institute's environmental justice programs in 14 high schools in metropolitan Boston to the national YMCA's Earth Service Corps, a key forerunner of the Y's own reenergized movement for democracy. State service commissions provide infrastructure for funding, technical assistance, and collaboration across the broad field of community service, including adult and senior volunteers, and are represented by the American Association of State Service Commissions in Washington, D.C.

Still other networks promote various practices of peer leadership, peer mediation, youth philanthropy, and youth organizing. National and state networks in peer leadership and peer mediation have developed important practices for youth engagement in problem solving in schools and communities. The Medical Foundation, for instance, has used peer leadership models in its work on community health education on tobacco and AIDS through the Massachusetts prevention centers and has built partnerships with Boys and Girls Clubs, YMCAs, and schools to empower young people in this process. The burgeoning practice of "youth philanthropy," through which young people themselves are actively engaged in mapping community assets and making decisions about grants for youth development and other projects, receives support from various national foundations, the Coalition of Community Foundations for Youth, and centers such as the Youth Leadership Institute and the Center for Youth as Resources. Increasingly, youth have also become actively engaged in community evaluation and research.

The Funders' Collaborative on Youth Organizing fosters the development of models that combine community organizing and youth development, especially among low-income youth and youth of color, in addressing such issues as criminal justice, public education, identity politics, and environmental justice. Some groups, such as the Boston-area Youth Organizing Project, modeled on faith-based relational organizing principles, have chapters in churches, synagogues, and schools, while others draw more on classic Alinsky methods, albeit often with heavier doses of political education. Other national projects, such as the Youth Leadership for Development Initiative and Lifting New Voices, have also been directed at youth organizing, as are intermediary organizations such as the Center for Community Change, Movement Strategy Center, and LISTEN, Inc.

Civic Education

While the community youth development movement has emerged largely in response to the limits of the deficits-driven model of youth services, the renewed interest in civic education has several other sources. First and foremost is that, amidst all the general concern about declining social capital in the United States, young people show the most serious disengagement from politics, as measured in terms of voting, campaign activities, political knowledge, interest in public affairs, and trust in fellow citizens. While a gap has always existed between youth and adult political participation, it has widened in recent years. And as young people grow older, they have not been increasing their participation at the rates of previous generations. Second, increases in community service by young people, notable in recent years, do not automatically translate into political engagement and in some cases might actually contribute to a withdrawal from politics. And, third, it seems clear that schools have contributed to youth disengagement by their general neglect of civic education for the past three or four decades. An increasing body of research and practice now shows that civic knowledge matters for the vitality of public life, and that civic education can, if well designed, increase the quantity and quality of civic knowledge and enhance the propensity of young people to become engaged and competent civic actors.

The Civic Mission of Schools (2003), a joint publication of the Carnegie Corporation of New York and the Center for Information and Research on Civic Learning and Engagement (CIRCLE), draws on the contributions of a wide range of innovative civic education practitioners and researchers in establishing a broad conceptual frame and policy agenda. It advocates that schools play a critical role in civic education since they reach virtually all young people and possess the capacity to engage students in the cognitive aspects of good citizenship. Schools can teach the ideas and principles essential to a constitutional democracy and combine these with active learning opportunities, such as simulations, mock trials and elections, participation in student government, collaborative action research projects, and service learning. A civic mission can be infused into the curriculum, as well as extracurricular activities, classroom culture, and even school governance—though the last is one of the few issues about which the report's endorsers did not reach consensus. Active discussions that link public issues to students' lives in their communities, and to local as well as state and federal levels of government, prove especially effective.

The service-learning movement in K–12 education has been refining the experiential learning component of this larger frame for about 15 years. The *Essential Elements of Service Learning*, developed by the National Service-Learning Cooperative in 1999, has become accepted by leading practitioners and widely disseminated. These guidelines include not only having clear educational goals and assessment, but also addressing community needs with work of consequence, forming genuine partnerships with the community, and including student voice in selecting, designing, implementing, and evaluating service projects. The National Commission on Service Learning's final report, *Learning In Deed: The Power of Service Learning for America's Schools* (2002), endorses these guidelines and elaborates an action agenda to reclaim the public purposes of education; increase the policy, program, and financial supports for K–12 service learning; and develop a comprehensive system of professional development to foster it. *Learning In Deed* also notably endorses giving students real authority, responsibility, and accountability for developing service-learning initiatives at all levels—school, district, state, and national—and helping them develop the leadership networks to make this possible.

Service learning has grown substantially in the past two decades. In 1984, only an estimated 900,000 K–12 students enrolled in service-learning courses nationally, whereas in 2004 this number had risen to 4.7 million students in some 23,000 public schools. This estimate follows more rigorous definitional standards introduced in 1999 (such as action to address real community needs in a sustained manner over a period of time, clearly stated learning objectives, and organized academic reflection and lesson drawing). By looser standards, the number may be as high as 12 million students. While unevenness characterizes the quality of these service-learning offerings and many research questions still need to be answered, the body of evidence available is very promising. Not only can well-designed service-learning programs contribute to academic learning and personal development, but they can also enhance students' awareness of community needs, confidence that they can make a difference, political knowledge and attentiveness, propensity to vote, and likelihood that they will participate in community organizations 15 years later.

Civic Education and Service-Learning Networks

The organizational networks involved in efforts to strengthen civic education broadly, and service learning more specifically, are now very extensive, have substantial overlap, and reach into many of the most important educational associations in the country. The National Service-Learning Partnership, formed in 2001 as a national leadership and advocacy organization, includes more than 8,000 individual and organizational members. Like the National Commission on Service Learning, it grew out of the Learning In Deed initiative of the Kellogg Foundation, which has invested heavily in many service-learning and youth leadership projects for more than a decade. The partnership, housed at the Academy for Educational Development, also administers the Youth Innovation Fund to promote youth-directed civic action linked to service learning through a range of partnership configurations among school systems, youth development agencies, youth commissions, community organizing groups, city agencies for children and youth, and other organizations. Eight cities currently participate in this project to raise youth civic engagement to a new level of sustainability.

The National Alliance for Civic Education (NACE), established in 2000, played an important role in initially bringing together some 200 individual and organizational members, including the most prominent national centers that provide curriculum and training, professional associations of educators, university institutes, and state education and legislative groups. The Center for Civic Education is coordinating a campaign with the National Conference of State Legislatures and the Center for Congress at Indiana University to promote civic education in all 50 states. CIRCLE, set up at the University of Maryland in 2001 as part of a larger youth civic engagement strategy of the Pew Charitable Trusts, has supported research with the intention of furthering innovative practice and shaping the public consciousness and policy agenda. CIRCLE's collaboration with the Carnegie Corporation on *The Civic Mission of Schools* has brought together networks across the ideological and disciplinary spectrum and has generated substantial consensus in a field that had previously been divided. This has helped inspire a new national movement for civic education, which includes important links to the community youth development movement as well. The recently launched Campaign for the Civic Mission of Schools, coordinated by the Center for Democracy and Citizenship at the

Council for Excellence in Government, is working with statewide coalitions that share a comprehensive approach to civic learning, which links the classroom to a broad range of experiential activities in communities. The steering committee of the campaign includes virtually all major organizations in the field.

The National Center for Learning and Citizenship at the Education Commission of the States assists state and district policymakers and educators in learning from best practices and developing policies that support civic education and service learning. The center also manages the Learning In Deed policy and practice demonstration project in five states to integrate service learning more fully into the K–12 curriculum. Its campaign, Every Student a Citizen: Creating the Democratic Self, which grew out of the National Study Group on Citizenship in K–12 Schools funded by the Ford Foundation, has promoted a robust conception of the "craft" of civic engagement and deep culture change that involves the collaboration of all stakeholders in the school (teachers, administrators, staff, parents, students, community members). It also promotes the idea that PTAs and PTOs should be reconfigured as Parent, Teacher, Student Associations/Organizations.

The resources to support and disseminate best practices, evaluation, and research have multiplied considerably in recent years through annual conferences on service learning, as well as through the activities of national centers and institutes for curriculum development and training, such as the Constitutional Rights Foundation, Center for Civic Education, Street Law, Public Achievement, Close Up Foundation, Choices for the 21st Century Education Project, Earth Force, and Do Something. Professional support has come from organizations such as the National Council for the Social Studies, National Association of Secondary School Principals, American Political Science Association, American Association of Colleges for Teacher Education, North American Association for Environmental Education, Council of Chief State School Officers, American Bar Association's Division of Public Education, American

Society for Public Administration, and National Association of Schools of Public Affairs and Administration. The Council for Excellence in Government and the National Conference of State Legislatures have provided important links to public officials.

As in higher education, service learning in K–12 schools and community settings has received indispensable field-building support from Learn and Serve America at the Corporation for National Service. Support began under 1990 legislation and then was increased substantially under the 1993 National and Community Service Trust Act. Grants have especially helped build capacity through state departments of education, state commissions on national and community service, Indian tribes, and nonprofit organizations such as the YMCA. As noted earlier, Learn and Serve also supports the National Service-Learning Clearinghouse.

Youth Civic Engagement in Hampton, Virginia

In this medium-sized, moderate-income city, with a youth population that is 52 percent African American and 40 percent white, city leaders were prompted in 1990 to expand their economic development and "reinventing government" efforts to include young people. Convened as part of a multistakeholder collaborative planning process that gave birth to the Hampton Coalition for Youth, a group of 20 young people told adults, in no uncertain terms, that they were tired of being viewed as broken and in constant need of fixing. They wanted to be challenged and provided substantial opportunities to contribute to the community.

This marked the beginning of a process that has matured into a citywide system for youth civic engagement that views young people as assets, not deficits. Adult stakeholders in the collaborative planning process agreed that the first principle of their vision was to "empower youth"; they saw their responsibility as providing a "comprehensive system of opportunities for youth to be involved in the life of the community." The city's leading nonprofit youth development agency, Alternatives, Inc., nationally renowned for its substance abuse prevention programs, reinvented itself under the leadership of Richard Goll to focus on training and mentoring youth for active engagement. With its first principle as "relationships, relationships, relationships," this reinvention became part of a larger organizing strategy within the community and government itself. The city formally recognized the Hampton Coalition for Youth as an office of city government with the mission to serve as a "learning community" and to spread best practices across city departments, including planning, police, parks and recreation, neighborhoods, and schools. Cindy Carlson, director of the coalition, refers to this as "our movement for youth civic engagement in Hampton."

The Hampton Youth Commission, 24 students from the city's four public and three private high schools, meets twice monthly to deliberate on a broad range of issues affecting youth. One meeting is an open public session at which youth commissioners sit in city council seats— often with a fully packed chamber of young people—to formulate strategies on such issues as developing a better racial climate in schools. Teenage "youth planners," part-time paid employees of the planning department who develop participatory planning for youth as part of the city's comprehensive plan, report to the youth commission. They have recommended, and the city council has subsequently approved, such initiatives as a multifunctional teen center with space designed by youth to represent their diverse interests and overall sense of ownership. Youth planners have also helped design a new bikeways system and improvements in bus services. Twice annually, the youth commission reports formally in televised sessions to the city council and planning commission.

Every month the superintendent of schools, along with the director of secondary education, meets with some 25 youths from the city's public high schools in the Superintendent's Advisory Group to discuss school policy. The meetings are facilitated by Alternatives staff and by highly trained youth leaders on the advisory group. School administrators display no sign of "professionals know best" but listen carefully and work collaboratively toward mutually acceptable solutions in an atmosphere that is at once thoughtfully deliberative and playfully energizing. The students also make periodic presentations to the city council, as well as to the city and state boards of education. Middle-school students also meet in their own superintendent's advisory group.

Each public high school has a principal's advisory group oriented toward policy and problem solving on a broad range of issues, including school safety, youth-to-youth mentoring, peer mediation, and social inclusion. At Kecoughtan High, for instance, the advisory group meets weekly; some 100 students are also active on various subcouncils. They have a voice in hiring teachers and guidance counselors. When students recognized the disservice, indeed injustice, done to school athletes by lackadaisical academic standards and then recommended a 2.0 GPA minimum for students to play on teams, they mobilized their own assets to help tutor and mentor them. Not one athlete has subsequently been disqualified from playing.

Recently, the Improving School Achievement committee at Kecoughtan High initiated a project on how to make classrooms more stimulating. Students interviewed teachers they respected and then classified their practices and attitudes into eight categories, such as ability to build relationships, manage the classroom, create high expectations, manage time, and engage students as resources in learning. The committee then published a booklet on how these practices could create a caring and learning environment. The principal agreed to use the booklet for teacher orientation at the beginning of the school year and to have youth serve as co-facilitators of training. In short, the everyday practical knowledge of students is not only deeply respected as a democratic resource, but is also mobilized to inform the professional practice of teachers.

Youth civic engagement has become part of the culture of city agencies. Alternatives have done extensive training with some agency staff to complement their leadership development among youth. Parks and Recreation involves young people in the planning of space, as well as the mediation of disputes with neighbors. The neighborhood commission also engages young people in planning at the neighborhood level and offers a "neighborhood/youth college" to help youth and adults develop the skills for working together. The police department has made real progress in getting officers to see themselves as "servants of young people" and to build relationships with them through "youth community policing" in the neighborhoods and as "resource officers" in the schools. Youth and police cowrote a curriculum for the police academy that embodies these principles and practices.

One indication of the diffusion of the culture of youth civic engagement is provided by a major (retired) in the police department. His eldest daughter was one of the 20 young people who helped develop the original strategy for youth engagement in the city in 1990. Another daughter had been active in an antidrug campaign. In 2002, his son was serving on the school superintendent's advisory group.

Healthy Communities

I n 1988, the U.S. Public Health Service's Office of Disease Prevention and Health Promotion provided funds for the National Civic League to develop a Healthy Communities Initiative that would catalyze many different kinds of institutional and civic partnerships to improve health status and to engage citizens directly in creating their own vision of a healthy community. Innovators drew not only on World Health Organization models from Toronto and Europe, but also on community-based and self-help efforts of the previous decades. These included the community health centers movement, women's health movement, disability and independent living movements, health decisions movement, AIDS/HIV organizing and care, and the federally mandated Health Systems Agencies, which mobilized new community actors in participatory health planning from the mid-1970s through the mid-1980s. Over the past decade, the healthy communities movement has enriched civic practice in the health arena but has also encountered more serious obstacles than in some other arenas.

Coproducing Health: A Broad View

The healthy communities frame takes a broad view of health as including much more than medical care. Health is produced not only by medical professionals, but also by a wide range of other institutional and civic actors. People become healthier not merely when they have access to medical services, as essential as these are, but also when they live in vibrant neighborhoods, reside in decent housing, and work in safe places. They grow healthier when they have cultural norms that support healthy behaviors and lifestyle choices and can draw on supportive family, peer, and social networks, including faith-based ones.

They also become healthier when urban design and transport encourages active living and when recreational facilities are broadly available. And, indeed, citizens are too often unhealthy because these social and cultural resources are unavailable or are distributed in highly unequal ways. Neither acute medical care nor overspecialization within the public health system itself can adequately address these issues. In view of the innumerable behavioral, social, and environmental factors that impact health, as so much epidemiological research now shows, creating healthy individuals means cultivating healthy communities.

This view of health has led many health innovators to design new kinds of partnerships among health care institutions and community actors. It has also led to a convergence with other innovative civic approaches, including assets-based community development, community visioning, community youth development, community policing, environmental justice, and sustainable communities. As Tyler Norris, former director of the Coalition for Healthier Cities and Communities, has argued, the healthy communities movement seeks to establish that it is not only medical providers but also "we—citizens—who are the producers of health."

The healthy communities coalition in Aiken, South Carolina, a small city hard hit by defense cuts in the 1990s, involved some 300 citizens in a two-year visioning and strategic planning process, using the National Civic League's *Civic Index* and McKnight and Kretzmann's asset mapping. Its Growing Into Life task force involved some 62 civic associations and government agencies, from the Junior Women's League and the Breastfeeding Association to Head Start and Clemson University, in a very successful effort to reduce high infant mortality rates and then addressed teen pregnancy and domestic and child abuse. Community policing teams, trained by public health nurses, became critical links in outreach and information in this process, which helped the city win several "innovations in government" awards. Police officers then extended their work to broader issues of health and safety, such as the supply and use of smoke detectors and fire extinguishers, water safety for kids, and programs for seniors to protect them from illegal scams and help them with prescription medicine safety. The police used their own asset of a small office in a housing project to persuade the housing authority to contract for a local on-site clinic. They also collaborated with other agencies and local residents to streamline enforcement of housing codes, get dangerous buildings demolished, and clean up several hundred unsightly lots.

The Solano Coalition for Better Health, extending across seven cities in Solano County, California, initially grew out of the efforts of a group of local physicians, hospital administrators, and county officials to prevent the closure of a primary care clinic that served low-income residents. As various other partners, including Kaiser Permanente, joined the collaboration, the Solano Partnership Healthplan emerged to serve MediCal (Medicaid) beneficiaries. Drawing on the model of its innovative community outreach in Hawaii, Kaiser developed field teams of community health outreach workers, each headed by a public health nurse, to provide education in prevention, to build family capacity for self-help, and to link families to primary care providers. Kaiser and other partners helped organize a community health training center at Solano Community College to train these teams, as well as members of neighborhood health councils, who were also provided civic leadership training. A Community Services Task Force brought together an interagency group of other health and social service providers, nonprofit and school district providers, neighborhood associations and advocates of ethnic groups and special populations. As the partnership circle widened, a broader definition of community health took hold.

In Boston, the commissioner of the city's Department of Health and Hospitals teamed up with the mayor, who had a strong track record in neighborhood empowerment, to develop Healthy Boston, which included 21 local coalitions by the summer of 1993. Each was required to have diverse participation among social and ethnic groups, as well as representatives from five types of actors: health, education, economic development, housing, and human services. The Gay, Lesbian, Bisexual and Transgender Youth group was the major coalition not identified with a specific neighborhood. Efforts were directed at identifying and developing new leadership through church and other community groups. The coalitions engaged in a number of citywide projects, such as Kids Can't Fly to increase the use of window guards and the Speak Easy Program to enhance English skills and develop a health curriculum to be used by teachers of English to Speakers of Other Languages (ESOL). They participated in a local partnership with Health Care for All and the Mayor's Health Line to enroll uninsured children in a no- or low-cost plan, and the coalitions worked with the community health centers and other institutional partners to disseminate the latest health statistics for specific neighborhoods.

Local coalitions also collaborated in the strategic planning process of the Boston Police Department, which had launched what was to become a very successful community-policing effort to reduce youth violence. These coalitions engaged in a great variety of projects on health education and prevention for domestic violence, smoking, asthma, teen pregnancy, breast cancer, substance abuse, obesity, and HIV/AIDS. They coordinated gun buy-back initiatives, organized neighborhood crime watches and safe houses, collaborated in immunization programs, and sponsored many other community improvement efforts such as community gardens, youth centers, teen mediation programs, and job-training fairs. The Allston-Brighton coalition combined its ESOL work with the development of community-organizing skills among its increasingly heterogeneous population. In other cases, the coalitions served as the civic infrastructure for related projects funded by prominent national and local foundations, as well as by state and federal grants. They tended to develop expansive notions about community health that included enhanced social connectedness and leadership development, rather than the narrow delivery of services.

State and National Networks

The late 1990s witnessed the formation of statewide healthy community projects and coalitions in as many as 34 states, several of which had relatively well developed infrastructures. One of the more ambitious state initiatives emerged in South Carolina through a partnership of the South Carolina Hospital Association and the South Carolina Department of Health and Environmental Control. Other state partners were added along the way, including the South Carolina Christian Action Council, Department of Health and Human Services, Municipal Association, Downtown Development Association, and Area Health Education Consortium. The hospitals tithed one million dollars to support community visioning work and the training of multisectoral teams in the majority of counties, such as Aiken, whose work we discussed above.

The Healthy Communities Initiative in South Carolina developed an expansive vision. If the health behavior of individuals is greatly influenced by their social, economic, political, and environmental contexts, then systematic improvement requires organizing. In this model, health practitioners identify and develop community leaders who can define their own problems and assume ownership of strategies, including coalition-building, policy, and media advocacy. "In many ways the practitioner's function is to produce community organizers." It is *"not* to 'do,' but to 'enable.' *Health practitioners serve as facilitators while the community does the work,"* according to the official vision statement.

Healthy Communities Massachusetts built on the work of Healthy Boston, as well as that of the Area Health Education Center/Community Partners in Western Massachusetts, and now continues its community-based training and visioning work through the regional prevention centers funded by the state's Department of Public Health. California Healthy Cities and Communities began as a collaboration of the Department of Health Services and the Western Consortium for Public Health and is now managed through the Center for Civic Partnerships at the Public Health Institute in Sacramento. The initiative has engaged some 60 cities and communities in developing official healthy city plans and a broad array of projects from youth violence and injury prevention to tobacco control and immigrant health. The Colorado Healthy Communities Initiative was established by a grant from the Colorado Trust, a conversion foundation set up with the proceeds from the sale of the Presbyterian/St. Luke's Medical Center in Denver. CHCI was directed in its early years by the National Civic League and helped to build core groups in several dozen communities, ranging from a small inner-city neighborhood to large multicounty areas. It developed a statewide council to work with legislators on policy development, based on community health indicator profiles generated through citizen participation in many communities.

Several national organizations have been especially important to the development of the healthy communities movement. The National Civic League, as noted above, directed the first national initiative to provide critical training and other resources to state networks and local innovators. It bought a distinctively civic frame to a movement that included many health care institutions and professionals whose main orientation has been service integration or specific public health issues. NCL helped connect health professionals to local government and civic innovators through its publications, national conferences, and All-America City Awards program. The Hospital Research Education Trust (HRET) of the American Hospital Association has provided critical institutional support. HRET also housed the Community Care Networks (CCN) Demonstration Program, funded by the Kellogg Foundation, which permitted cross-fertilization between healthy communities and the 25 local and regional partnerships within CCN. The Healthcare Forum, now also part of HRET, helped enhance the movement through its annual healthy communities summits, fellowships, and best-practices forums and guide.

The Centers for Disease Control and Prevention have produced a variety of resources for public health professionals in local and state health departments to guide their work in community-based health planning, assets mobilization, and local leadership development. The Interfaith Health Program, originally at the Carter Center and now at Emory University, has helped develop models of healthy community collaborations that involve religious institutions in several metropolitan areas, as well as through national ministerial and parish nursing associations and five higher education Faith and Health Consortia, which include schools of medicine, nursing, public health, social work, and seminaries. A Caucus on Public Health and Faith Communities within the American Public Health Association also lends support to a "faith and health movement."

In 1996, leaders from these and other organizations joined to form the Coalition for Healthier Cities and Communities as a national movement center. Expanding its membership to more than one thousand organizations and individuals, the coalition helped catalyze additional state networks and policy development. However, as a result of funding pressures on HRET and an inability to secure its own funds, the coalition disbanded in 2002. Some of its key leaders, as well as those from CCN, have joined the new Association for Community Health Improvement (ACHI), also housed at HRET. It is unclear how much this association will be able to provide new momentum to the healthy communities movement, which has also experienced some notable setbacks in state networks, as well as the narrowing of civic practices in local coalitions such as Solano. The national coalition's demise, however, has prompted serious reflection on some of the inherent tensions and limits of the movement that many had recognized for quite some time.

Public Journalism and Civic Communications

T he "public journalism movement" (also known as "civic journalism") emerged in the United States in the early 1990s and grew into what one prominent sociologist referred to as "the best organized social movement inside journalism in the history of the American press." Public journalism arose in response to an increasingly pervasive sense among journalists that the press was becoming dangerously disconnected from civic life. The movement spread through a network of newspapers, foundations, and academics, refining its broad objectives and inventing new journalistic methods. By 2002, over a fifth of all U.S. newspapers had experimented with distinctively civic journalistic practices. During the late 1990s, other civic innovations in communication also began to emerge. The "information commons movement" responds to the needs of local communities for new forms of shared knowledge. New models of "interactive journalism" or "participatory journalism," stimulated by the World Wide Web, have also begun to spread. These sometimes draw directly from public journalism practice, but they are also inventing some distinct forms of civic news coverage.

Principles of Public Journalism

The philosophy of public journalism, as manifest in the writings of its leading theorists and practitioners, can be summarized as follows: Journalists must assume responsibility for helping to constitute vital "publics" with the usable knowledge that enables them to deliberate about complex issues and to engage in collective problem solving. Since journalists invariably frame and narrate the stories of our common life in reporting "the facts," they should do so with an eye to how their stories permit people to build knowledge and see themselves as citizens, rather than as mere spectators, victims, or consumers of information. While civic journalists should not compromise their objectivity through advocacy journalism or by taking the lead in developing solutions to problems, they can play convening and catalytic roles that bring citizens together to deliberate among themselves and with those who hold positions of power so that citizens may help fashion strategies for solving public problems.

To expand citizens' knowledge of potentially useful models and to generate a sense of efficacy, journalists can also shine a comparative spotlight on solutions that seem to work reasonably well in other communities. Journalists should not advocate for specific models or succumb to feel-good news and superficial optimism. Indeed, public journalists can be tough on those in power by challenging them to respond to citizens' agendas and real-life concerns and by holding them accountable for their responses. Finally, public journalists must hold citizens themselves accountable for grappling with the full complexity of issues and acting responsibly to solve common problems. The emphasis of public journalism is on the democratic work of citizens in a self-governing republic and on the vital role of journalists as "civic professionals" in facilitating informed public discourse to enable citizens to do this work effectively.

Traditional journalism has incorporated some of these practices, especially with the rise of the civic journalism movement. Yet it has tended to focus on the horse race aspects of politics, holding that the press does not bear responsibility for the quality or direction of public life, but only for accurately reporting conflict within it. Even while the traditional press depends on the health

of community and civic life for its core business, it has sometimes renounced responsibility for helping make civic life go
well. And with the rise of corporate concentration across all
media, the substitution of entertainment for news values and a
focus on the economies to be gained from digital convergence,
the mainstream, privately owned media has too often in recent
years turned away from public values that it once recognized.

The Public Journalism Movement

The public journalism movement grew initially out of the
Knight-Ridder newspaper chain, led by CEO James K. Batten.
Concerned about declining readership and the drift of newspapers from their communities, Batten began a companywide
search for new forms of "community connectedness" in the
late 1980s. In a series of experiments, beginning in Columbus,
Georgia, in 1987 and moving soon to Wichita, Kansas, and
Charlotte, North Carolina, editors at Knight-Ridder papers
began to wrestle with the relationship between their coverage
and democracy. In addition, national civic leaders, such as John
Gardner, who would help initiate a broad civic renewal movement over the next several years, enabled journalists and editors
to rethink their relationship to communities.

The practices of public journalism vary, but there has been
considerable mutual learning across news organizations as the
result of movement efforts. In Wichita, Davis "Buzz" Merritt,
editor of the Knight-owned *Wichita Eagle,* responded to what he
saw as a breakdown in the fundamental relationship between
the press and the public. Merritt and the *Eagle* experimented
with a new model of "citizen-driven" election coverage of the
1990 Kansas gubernatorial race. After polling citizens on the
issues most important to them, journalists asked questions of
the candidates—who quickly learned to answer the citizen
questions, even if they preferred the old way of doing things.

Strong citizen-reader response drove the project forward. By 1992, the *Eagle* sought to expand the experiment from politics to civic life and launched "The People Project: Solving It Ourselves." This project responded to a recurring theme the reporters had not initially expected to hear in the community: maybe the problems are not just the government's responsibility, and maybe we have to assume our rightful responsibility as citizens to solve them. The People Project explored a series of problems facing Wichita and sought citizen-solutions through a new kind of public deliberation in the pages of the newspaper. This civic journalism project also proved very successful and had a strong indirect effect on local public life, spawning the Wichita Neighborhood Initiative, a deliberative democracy project, and Wichita Independent Neighborhoods, a communitywide organization.

The Knight-owned *Charlotte Observer* (which Batten had once edited) tackled early election projects in 1992 and then, in 1994, launched "Taking Back Our Neighborhoods" under the leadership of editor Jennie Buckner. This path-breaking effort to link coverage of crime to its underlying causes included extensive neighborhood forums on problems and potential solutions. These forums were followed by intensive, coordinated coverage by television and radio partners for more than a year and included spotlights on successful strategies in other communities in Charlotte and around the country. The media partners also covered citizen and governmental efforts to implement solutions.

"Taking Back Our Neighborhoods" brought about lasting changes in the neighborhoods and the wider metropolitan community, as well as in the newspaper itself. The project helped to forge civic linkages across lines of class, race, and neighborhood and was widely credited by citizens, government, and police officials with helping reduce crime in the most dangerous neighborhoods, as well as with the mobilization of communitywide social capital. Magnet schools opened their doors to the neighborhoods for after-school programs. Community centers were established where children could be tutored, and school supplies, uniforms, and recreational equipment were collected and distributed. Neighborhood leaders began to meet with each other, in some cases for the first time, thereby engendering new forms of grass-roots engagement and leadership training.

After the project, the *Charlotte Observer* continued its efforts with shorter daily and weekly civic series on race, education, the environment, and many other topics. The paper was reorganized into beats with a broad civic framing of issues. By 2000, it had become the most consistent civic newsroom in the United States, although it had largely abandoned the explicit rhetoric of civic journalism.

In Madison, Wisconsin, the "We, the People Project," launched in 1991, enriched the democratic culture of Madison and Wisconsin communities statewide with a series of innovative collaborations among Wisconsin Public Television, Wisconsin Public Radio, the *Wisconsin State Journal,* CBS affiliate WISC-TV (Madison), and a local public relations firm. The project reported on both critical state elections and public issues, such as taxes, health care, budgets, land use, and the environment. In-depth issues reporting by each of the media partners was typically combined with careful community-based deliberation and then followed by regional or statewide on-air coverage that featured innovative techniques of citizen reporting, questioning, or small-group deliberation. By the late 1990s, to "we-the-people" an issue had become a transitive verb in Wisconsin political culture. Today, it remains the oldest continuing civic journalism project in the nation.

In Norfolk, Virginia, and the surrounding "Hampton Roads" cities, the *Virginian-Pilot* undertook an ambitious effort to build capacity for daily civic reporting. The newspaper initiated a series of innovations, including "community conversations" and "public life pages," designed, in the words of former managing editor Dennis Hartig, to do "public work" that "builds capacity" in the Norfolk region. "Capacity—public knowledge—will come about from routines and disciplines driven by very simple questions. 'What is political knowledge?' 'What is the political information that people need day in and day out to function effectively in communities and with their neighbors?'"

For several years, the *Pilot* mapped a civic agenda in its five-city area on the topics of government, education, and public safety. Each topic had a carefully formatted weekly public life page designed to build public memory on local issues, leading to better civic deliberation and decision making. For example, a segment on a new library proposal in Virginia Beach would be accompanied by earlier proposals and their fate and comparisons with surrounding communities. These would be followed by short informative follow-ups, sometimes only a paragraph long, on how the project was moving through the decision-making process. Citizens reported that, although they hadn't read the paper before, or read only the sports pages, they had begun photocopying articles and distributing them in their neighborhoods and through civic organizations. The public life pages motivated citizens to become involved and attend trainings, and the civic institutions in turn taught citizens how to use the newspaper in a public way.

National Networks

Almost all of these efforts were supported in some way by the Project on Public Life and the Press (PPLP) and the Pew Center for Civic Journalism (PCCJ). The PPLP, founded by New York University professor Jay Rosen in 1993 and funded by the Knight Foundation, served as a center for practical research and reflection until it closed in 1997. It served as a think tank for the movement, as executive and midlevel editors, senior reporters, and new hires mingled with leading journalism scholars in quarterly seminars at the American Press Institute in Reston, Virginia. The seminars helped revive John Dewey's long-forgotten work on the public and the press, thereby forging a language that connected the practical concerns of the newsroom and larger questions of democratic theory.

The Pew Center, founded by Ed Fouhy in 1994 and later directed by Jan Schaffer, took a slightly different approach. Both were experienced, award-winning journalists. Their primary goal was to set up a series of newsroom experiments whose results could be studied, publicized, and replicated. The PCCJ awarded annual grants to news organizations and also served as a center for reflection on practice and technique through scores of workshops and a clearinghouse of ideas until it closed in 2002. The Pew Center eventually reached out to many hundreds of newsrooms, both directly and through important journalism organizations like the American Society of Newspaper Editors and Investigative Reporters and Editors. Our own study, which systematically analyzed the Pew archives, found that 320 American newspapers, approximately one-fifth of the total, had conducted almost 650 civic journalism projects from 1994 to 2001.

By 2002, however, there was a sense that the momentum in the civic journalism movement had ground almost to a halt or had shifted to new areas of interactive media (discussed below). In Madison, for instance, the rigors of coordinating "We, the People" took its toll on the original leaders and by 2000 most had moved on to other activities, although the partnership remained. By 2001, in Norfolk, the public life pages were abandoned and many key editors and reporters had left for academia or other newspapers.

Several factors account for the decline of public journalism. First, it became difficult to sustain the movement against its opposition. From its inception, mainstream press critics and press reviews generally reacted with hostility to civic journalism, even while many of its practices were being incorporated into the daily news report and even though civic journalists responded in compelling fashion to some of the most egregious misrepresentations of their practice. Unrelenting criticism that public journalism compromised traditional journalism's core values took its toll in the broader news community. Within newsrooms, advocates became tired of defending civic journalism and, in some cases, simply continued the practices without attempting to articulate them in terms of democratic renewal. This worked for several years, but the legitimacy and distinctiveness of the movement then began to fade, and what was left was a collection of new practices without a larger frame. Intellectual and academic leaders moved on to other activities, and many newsroom leaders, editors, and others went into the academy or simply became exhausted. Second, the generation of corporate leadership represented by James Batten passed, and leading corporate sponsors such as Knight-Ridder continued verbal support but became more focused on the bottom line in the face of the considerable costs of doing public journalism well and competing investments in new technologies. The Pew Center, the leading funder of civic journalism as well as its major organizer and disseminator of materials and best practices by the end of the 1990s, closed its doors in 2002, leaving a void that could not be filled by voluntary efforts.

When the Pew Center closed, and both financial and organizing support was withdrawn from the movement, there was a palpable sense that the civic journalism movement would be difficult to sustain. Major pockets of practice remain in newspapers edited by movement veterans. As noted, the *Charlotte Observer* continues much of its civic practice, although without naming it as such. The St. Paul *Pioneer Press,* the editorial pages of the Philadelphia *Inquirer,* the *Spokesman-Review* in Spokane, Savannah's *Morning News,* Memphis *Commercial-Appeal,* and Portland, Maine's, *Press Herald* are among the papers that actively continue this tradition.

Other newspapers that still incorporate elements of civic journalistic practice include the Orange County *Register,* Wichita *Eagle,* Tucson *Star,* San Jose *Mercury News,* Seattle *Times,* Philadelphia *Daily News,* and Portland *Oregonian,* along with dozens of smaller papers. In Tampa Bay, the *Tribune* has been a leader in digital convergence in the newsroom and still maintains a civic journalism tradition.

In the academic community, the Civic Journalism Interest Group remains active within the Association of Educators in Journalism and Mass Communication, the major scholarly organization of those who teach and research journalism. A national Public and Civic Journalism Archive has been established at the University of Wisconsin-Madison. In January 2003, academics and some practitioners formed the Public Journalism Network (PJNet) to continue active dialogue between practitioners and scholars. PJNet maintains an active Web site and Web log that cuts across multiple communities of practice and posts regular bulletins on developments in the movement. Finally, the Kettering Foundation, a key supporter from the beginning, has continued to convene meetings of journalism practitioners and scholars, seeking ways to deepen the relationships between them and to anchor the teaching of public journalism principles in the nation's journalism schools. Presuming that the movement might be revived under more favorable circumstances, these organizations can serve as "abeyance structures" not unfamiliar to other movements that have gone through periods of relative quiescence.

Civic Communications

Public journalism grew as a major, well-defined movement within the field of journalism. Civic communications as a field is both more extensive and less cohesive but has two broad branches: the information commons movement and new forms of citizen communication, including journalism. The "information commons movement" itself includes two broad but closely related subfields. The first focuses on local communities and their shared resources for communication, including both locally bounded cyberspace (for example, community Web portals) and physical spaces such as libraries, parks, streets, plazas, and other public spaces. The second branch of the information commons movement focuses on shared resources in information per se, including communication technology, software code, intellectual property, and the architecture of cyberspace. Other new forms of citizen communication on the Web are also rapidly emerging, often in loose partnership with commons advocates. Some forms are more purely Web-based, such as the networks of "blogs" that address public and civic themes. Others, such as integrated civic news portals run largely by nonprofits and citizens, echo and extend public journalism practices for the digital age.

The Information Commons Movement. The information commons movement is a growing network of groups united in the belief that citizens should enjoy access to the broadest possible range of information and communication as a "commons." The movement attracts a continuum of actors, ranging from those most concerned with using information to build public and civic space in local communities to those focused on building and strengthening the public and civic architecture of cyberspace as a whole. But commons advocates are not parochial; virtually all recognize that building local civic space is linked to the larger structure of information.

The commons language in communications first began to emerge in the mid-1990s and drew on research about the successful management of common-pool natural resources in land, water, and wildlife. This approach contrasted with "tragedy of the commons" theory, which suggested that the commons would necessarily be depleted or destroyed by free riders taking more than they contributed. Building on common-pool resource theory, advocates began to experiment with the idea of an "information commons." A Wingspread conference in early 2000 brought together leading organizers—librarians, youth advocates, public space activists, civic renewal and communication scholars, foundation leaders, and others—seeking ways to build common information spaces to enhance civic and public life in local communities.

University of Michigan researchers, for instance, established a model Community Information Corps. Professors and students in library and information science reflected on the emerging civic information needs of communities and, in Flint, Michigan, trained local citizens, especially young people, to gather and publish information about their neighborhoods. Building on this experiment, the Center for Democracy and Citizenship at the University of Minnesota and the Center for Communication and Democracy at the University of Wisconsin-Madison modeled a somewhat different Community Information Corps. The project recruited youth who had been exposed to Public Achievement in the Westside neighborhood of St. Paul. A multiracial group of Hmong, Latino, African American, and Caucasian young people interviewed more than 120 civic leaders in the community and identified key resources: citizenship and language instruction, day care, tutoring services, libraries, and others. These assets were mapped, using Geographic Information Systems technology, and served on a St. Paul Commons Web site built, in part, by the young Corps members themselves. The project was unveiled to the entire community and presented to the St. Paul School Board. Some collaboration was developed with the St. Paul *Pioneer Press*, a civic journalism-oriented newspaper, although the project was eventually folded into Public Achievement.

In Prince George's County, Maryland, scholar-activists in youth civic engagement built on the St. Paul experiments to create a Prince George's Information Commons in which young people gather local history, map and serve resources, create videos, and provide a community portal. The Prince George's project has also partnered with other agencies and nonprofits countywide to gain recognition for information commons interests, including governance models drawn, in part, from principles developed in common-pool resource models in other arenas. In Madison, Wisconsin, an experiment in civic mapping is developing a communitywide social capital database, as a collaborative effort among the Dane County United Way, WISC-TV (a civic journalism pioneer), the University of Wisconsin, and Edgewood College.

Beyond specific local commons efforts such as these, national organizations are seeking to establish local information commons space and to develop a larger democratic frame. The American Library Association (ALA), viewing libraries as common-space anchors in the community, has been a significant leader in this effort since the early 1990s. In 2001, the ALA also assumed leadership in the effort to bring about a national commons movement with a broader intellectual frame of information equity and public access, as well as a means for social experiment, diversity, and broad expression of democratic voice. Others emphasize the critical relationship of information architecture to full democratic participation and the development of new models of intellectual property in which knowledge is freely shared. The leadership of libraries, deliberative design of public spaces, and commons experiments indicate a growing commons movement in local communities.

The Information Commons: A Public Policy Report, by Nancy Kranich, outlines the most important components of the movement. Entire networks have emerged around specific aspects of the digital commons. *Software commons* designers have developed entire platforms, such as Linux, based on the free sharing of code and the core principles that user-communities should collaborate in the development of low-cost or free software in the public domain. An "open-source movement" is spreading through governments and universities as a way of building common wealth and freeing public agencies and civic organizations from dependence on large information corporations such as Microsoft. *Open Source* intellectual ventures such as WIKI, an on-line collaborative encyclopedia, and Project Gutenberg, through which contributors place works in the public domain on-line, represent broad citizen/nonprofit networks in which citizens contribute to the common good through cooperative information labor. Initiatives such as the Open Digital Rights Language, a collaboration among publishers, educators, and entertainment and software industries, are developing new commons-friendly language for digital rights management to ensure broad public access. The *General Public License* movement and *Creative Commons* create new legal forms of copyright that allow artistic creators, designers, and builders of intellectual property to place their work in the public domain while still retaining rights over their creations. *Open Access Scholarship* is challenging the quasi-monopoly of private publishers of scholarly journals over the work of scholars by developing new collaborative models of publishing with rigorous peer review and the sharing of journals on-line.

New Forms of Participatory Journalism. Cyberspace has also generated the impetus for innovative forms of "interactive" or "participatory" journalism, which some see as a new, more public form of journalism because it is open to nonprofessionals. Some forms of interactive journalism are quite traditional, essentially Web tools grafted onto the on-line sites of newspapers. Others, such as the growing world of blogs (or the "blogosphere"), create new voices in ways that challenge traditional journalism. Yet a third form, citizen-driven journalism on the Web, combines the most important elements of traditional journalism with the expansion of citizen voice and the scope of coverage.

Interactive journalism is spreading across the Web. Some of it cannot be characterized as civic per se but simply integrates new technologies such as e-mail and blogs to create quicker and easier feedback and communication between readers and news journals.

But J-Lab, the Institute for Interactive Journalism, established by Jan Schaffer, former director of the Pew Center for Civic Journalism, is promoting new forms of interaction that expand citizen knowledge on public policy and on-line deliberation. In 2000, the Pew Center seeded 16 interactive civic experiments, including the Washington *Everett-Herald's* project on smart growth, which allowed citizens to model their preferences for waterfront development. J-Lab promotes similar interactive policy games.

For example, citizens in Rochester, New York, can use the *Democrat and Chronicle's* interactive tax calculator to compare their taxes to those of other communities, as part of the "Fighting for Rochester's Future" Web site. In the civic journalism tradition, the site includes reporting and games on education, health care, and the economy. New Hampshire Public Radio pioneered citizen "gaming" on budget issues in 2002, when it launched an interactive "Budget Builder" that allowed citizens to make tradeoffs in the state budget (which was experiencing a deficit crisis) to see the relationship between choices and consequences. According to Schaffer, "Much of what I see happening on the Web really hails from the civic journalism playbook.... In the on-line games or news exercises, we're starting to see some impact on public policy—development plans tweaked, different tax scenarios considered, et cetera. I think it's showing the potential of serving as surrogate public hearings."

Some newspapers are also incorporating citizen voice in the form of blogs. At times, citizens become blog correspondents, extending the reach of the paper to neighborhoods and topic areas that otherwise would probably not be covered. The Spokane *Spokesman-Review,* a prominent civic journalism paper, has been an early leader in incorporating citizen blogging into its on-line coverage. Initially, citizens covered community events such as basketball games. Now the coverage has expanded to include blogs by reporters and editors on politics and religion, as well as reader-driven topics such as auto racing. Early public journalism leader Jay Rosen posts a national blog called "PressThink" and actively advocates blogging as a new form of participatory journalism that continues the public journalism tradition. He reasons that blogs are part of a gift economy (linking them to the commons movement) and barriers to entry are low. Readers and writers form an interlinked community; dialogue among small numbers of people is supportable; and information flows from the public to the press, rather than the other way around. Perhaps the most important rationale is that "Journalism traditionally assumes that democracy is what we have, information is what we seek. Whereas in the Web log world, information is what we have—it's all around us—and democracy is what we seek."

Clearly, blogs have opened an important new space for citizen participation and public voice, but critics argue that they represent a relatively closed circle of active readers and writers. While the participatory world of blogs is more open than traditional journalism, it is not necessarily more public. Although active bloggers monitor the mainstream press, looking for accuracy and ideological bias, the blogosphere has, in many respects, begun to reproduce an information space that is very divided and partisan. Advocates identify this as an important democratic role open to anyone with the time and talent to devote to it. Critics argue that the blogosphere fuels division, and in some cases rumor and character assassination, unconstrained by traditional journalistic norms and practices. Furthermore, because larger publics are not being addressed as they are in the traditional media, the blogosphere, while in principle open to all, remains a preserve of those with the time and resources to engage it actively. Nevertheless, we are beginning to see new forms of participatory, on-line, journalism that combine some of the best qualities of traditional journalism (addressing issues of public importance to large audiences), with the citizen voice of public journalism and the interactivity and openness of the blogging world. One of the most developed examples so far is the *Gotham Gazette* (see case profile).

The commons movement is growing rapidly. Libraries and other local nonprofits are recognizing that access to information represents a first step to a broader and deeper democratic discourse. New citizen journalists are no longer waiting for traditional news media to cover topics of vital concern to community and public life. Artists, writers, and musicians are joining with software designers, law professors, and other information commons activists to ensure that new forms of digital ownership are open and accessible to all citizens. The commons movement is seeking to develop new forms of property and production in information, which is absolutely critical to complex public problem solving. The movement sees this as an explicitly civic and democratic challenge, making it a significant component of an emerging civic renewal movement in an advanced information society.

The Gotham Gazette

The *Gotham Gazette* was founded in 1999 by the Citizens Union Foundation of New York, which works to promote an informed citizenry and participation in elections. The core purpose of the site is to provide "one-stop shopping for persons interested in the public policies and civic life of New York City" and to highlight leading "community groups, civic associations, and educational institutions, " from which many of its contributors are drawn. The site, which declares itself nonideological and nonpartisan, is supported through foundation grants and subscriptions.

Managed by editor Jonathan Mandell and a staff of four and a half, the *Gazette* publishes on-line every day (with a quarterly print edition). It is a unique combination of on-line newspaper, civic and arts portal, community news portal, and news digest. The center of the front page contains a daily news section, with links to recent state, education, finance, immigration, social services, and current debates (for example, the waterfront); and a set of links to organizations in government, non-profits, arts, labor, think tanks, and others. There are also links to sections on the five boroughs, as well as other sites for the New York media.

Readers can link to major subsections and special project. "The Citizen," a special section that digests news from New York's many immigrant papers and Web sites, is so named because all New Yorkers are citizens of the city, whatever their federal immigration status. We thus restore the word "citizen" to its root in the word "city." "Searchlight" provides a guide to New York government and politics. Another section "Rebuilding New York City," covers news, opinion, events calendars, and live chats about the recovery from 9/11; offers interactive civic games (for example, on the breakdown of city water, electricity, and phone systems); and features NYC bloggers. "Community Gazettes" cover news from each neighborhood in the five boroughs. Interns have written some neighborhood stories, for example, on firehouse closings and conflicts between landmark preservation commissions and local houses of worship. The *Gazette* also has several volunteer neighborhood moderators and is raising money to recruit a coordinator to find and train moderators in all 51 community districts covered by the *Gazette*.

The remarkable policy breadth of the *Gazette* is sustained by hundreds of citizen and public correspondents. (For example, 49 of the 51 city council members have written for the journal). A former staffer at *Life* magazine writes for the children's section and edits the newsletter of the Fifth Avenue Committee on public schools. The former editor of the *Audubon Activist* contributes to the parks section. Correspondents include professors, activists, members of planning committees and task forces, current and former journalists, and just plain citizens. The *Gazette* represents a genuine information commons, a site for shared production and communication, rooted in local community, linking citizens from across the city on issues that concern them. A place for deliberative discourse and amusement, the *Gazette* draws on the best of the new technology to produce a sense of community that transcends neighborhood and class. In short, the *Gazette* represents a new model of citizens' journalism that constitutes a public space, a second wave that advances public journalism for the information age.

Part Two:

A Movement for Democratic Renewal

Why Innovation?

Why a Movement?

Civic Renewal as a
Movement Master Frame

That there has been noteworthy civic innovation in various arenas seems clear enough. But what is the larger significance of these innovations for democratic renewal?

In Part Two we first reprise some general factors behind innovation and then pose the question of why the United States needs an expansive movement crosscutting specific arenas and civic movements. We examine how a broad civic renewal movement has begun to emerge. Here we look specifically at the development of what social movement theorists call an "elaborated master frame" that establishes credible commonalties and complementarities among the various kinds of civic innovation and that links them to the larger challenge of revitalizing civil society, professional practice, and democratic institutions. While this master frame is largely one of pragmatic democracy that foregrounds coproduction and collaboration, it nonetheless must grapple with "rights" and "justice" rhetoric central to other democratic social movement frames.

Why Innovation?

C ivic innovation, as we have seen, occurs for many different reasons and according to dynamics specific to particular arenas of community and institutional life, public policy, and the kinds of public goods being produced. While there exists no singular logic or privileged organizational form, innovation generally occurs in response to some combination of the following factors:

- *Empowered and diverse citizens.* New civic actors enter the public arena, often with expanded rights and democratized knowledge that upset traditional ways of doing business. These actors not only find older forms of social capital and civic organization inadequate to the new challenges, but also come to recognize the limits of narrow public hearing formats, issue advocacy, and oppositional social movement organizing.

- *Adversarial stalemate.* Problem solving and public policy-making stalemate because adversaries lock themselves in combat and, as a result, pay high costs, such as prolonged court battles and extended uncertainty. After years of struggle, they may be winning the battles but losing the war. In addition, adversarialism in one arena can have negative spillover effects on the overall quality of community life and capacity to solve other problems.

- *Command-and-control regulation.* Regulation from above, while achieving important gains, often runs up against limits and spawns unintended consequences, especially when dealing with increased complexity and uncertainty. It cannot, by itself, generate enough context-specific knowledge, local initiative, or legitimacy to make long-term improvements and frequently compounds problems further.

- **Bureaucratic service delivery.** Bureaucratic power, especially of those invoking clinical authority over passive clients, proves unable to mobilize enough community assets to solve problems and can contribute to patterns of long-term dependency. Bureaucratic service delivery and fragmented, categorical programs often create a "crazy quilt" with suboptimal results and low public legitimacy. Treating individuals and communities as bundles of deficits becomes a self-fulfilling prophecy.
- **Professional practice.** Whether as city planners, police officers, social workers, environmental regulators, or public health officials, professionals often employ practices that misdiagnose problems, invalidate other forms of knowledge, and disable the problem-solving capacities of ordinary people. As a result, they often fail to generate sufficient legitimacy and may deepen mistrust of public institutions.
- **Particularistic interests.** Interest representation, while critical to a pluralist democracy, often takes such narrow forms that it becomes difficult to discover and act on larger public purposes.

Responding to a mix of these and other factors in a specific arena, civic innovators develop a wide variety of forms for pragmatic problem solving, democratic deliberation, and community asset mobilization. They generate new sources of trust and elicit collaboration from actors and institutions previously segmented from each other or locked in combat. They redefine understandings of the common good and the interdependence of self-interests. Mobilizing new sources of knowledge and insight, innovators elicit many-sided contributions for coproducing public goods. In some cases, they work within a broad vision of renewed democracy. In arenas such as higher education and K–12 civic education, their larger democratic purpose is often quite explicit and expansive, since they are responding directly to indicators of civic decline, such as the disengagement of young people from public life.

Scholars, of course, have analyzed various causes of civic decline. Some causes are perhaps reversible, but others may represent permanent shifts in cultural and institutional life. For Robert Putnam, the replacement of the generation whose civic identities were formed in the WW II era of national unity and patriotism, along with the technological shift in leisure that leads to the privatized habits associated with the television and CD player, are major causes of decline in overall aggregates of social capital. In addition, the increasing movement of women into the labor force makes them less available for community activities, and commuting and urban sprawl draw many people away from local involvements.

For Theda Skocpol, the most worrisome shift has been the decline in multitiered and cross-class mass membership organizations, such as the Odd Fellows, Federation of Women's Clubs, Grange, and American Legion. These associations once used to link local participation and leadership development with state and national capacities for advocacy. Their decline stems from a variety of factors, such as more egalitarian gender and racial norms that undermined the traditional solidarities based on gender and racial segregation within these associations, as well as the eclipse in patriotic brotherhood due to the Vietnam War and the professionalization of the military. Educated women, previously key leaders in cross-class associations, have shifted their involvements increasingly to professional societies. Furthermore, since the 1960s, new political and media opportunities in Washington, D.C., and new sources of direct-mail and foundation

funding have placed a premium on staff-driven advocacy domi-
nated by middle-class elites who have little reason to enlist active
mass memberships.

Other scholars stress different factors in the decline of social
capital and trust, for example, increasing economic inequality,
ethnic heterogeneity, metropolitan fragmentation, and heightened
individualism and materialism among young people. All of these
explanations have considerable merit, to be sure.

But even if one takes a less alarmist view of civic decline, it is
nonetheless important to recognize that American society needs
to revitalize and modernize its civic infrastructure over the
coming decades if it is to successfully address the increasingly
complex problems of a world undergoing rapid transformation.
Thus, it is perhaps more appropriate to speak of the "civic
challenge" rather than "civic decline" or "civic crisis." Facing
increasingly complex problems and ever more diverse actors
and interests in a highly differentiated society, we will require
new organizational and institutional capacities for collaborative
problem solving and public work in the decades ahead. The growing complexity, scale, and social differentiation of postmodern
societies generate increasing policy problems for which regulatory
enforcement, programmatic entitlement, market incentive, and
professional intervention prove inadequate unless coupled with
new forms of civic trust, cooperation, deliberation, and learning.

Many older forms of social capital tend to be devalued in the
face of increased complexity and social differentiation, which raise
the relative requirements of citizen expertise needed to solve
problems, widen the scope of network relationships that must be
brought to bear, and increase the cognitive preconditions for trust
building. In other words, citizens and civic organizations need
much greater knowledge and capacity to learn amidst uncertainty;
they need to interact with a broader array of stakeholders
unlike themselves; and they need to learn to build trust while

monitoring the behavior of those who have many incentives to act opportunistically and with whom they might regularly come into conflict. As increasing social complexity fosters the growth of the administrative state, it becomes especially important to design "policy for democracy" and "empowered participatory governance" so that public policy and administration serve to empower, enlighten, and engage citizens in the process of self-government, rather than further eroding civic capacities.

Increasing the aggregate levels of social capital, from socializing to churchgoing (as Putnam recommends in *Bowling Alone*), will do little to add to capacities for democratic governance unless we also invest substantially in specific forms of civic innovation that engage diverse stakeholders in robust problem solving and copro-duction. Multitiered mass membership associations, if it is possible to reconstitute them or create functional equivalents (as Skocpol suggests), will help revitalize democracy only to the extent that their lower tiers likewise engage in innovative problem solving and complex multistakeholder partnerships and their upper-tier state and national advocacy incorporates "policy design for democracy" to enable complex public work. Neither of these features were hallmarks of the classic American associations during their heyday. Thus, neither general social capital strategies nor specific reforms aimed at reconstituting multitiered mass membership associations can avoid the lessons of the kinds of civic innovation that have emerged in recent years, even if these innovations are quite incomplete in their current forms.

In short, it is much more difficult for Americans to be effective citizens today than it was 50 years ago. Indeed, this might be why some people have withdrawn from public life. We need to gain greater expertise and find new ways to work with experts without subordinating ourselves to them. We need to collaborate with a broader range of stakeholders and negotiate increasingly diverse interests to mutual satisfaction. We must develop capacities for experimental and collaborative learning under conditions of increasing complexity and uncertainty in which civic and political actors are much more alert to the potential unintended consequences and perverse effects of policy instruments. We can no longer design public goods so that one size fits all. We can no longer remain insulated in old residential or ethnic neighborhoods or gender-and race-segregated associations but must deliberately create forms of social capital that bridge demographic, geographic, and institutional boundaries.

These challenges require upgraded civic skills and sustained capacity building. Just as our postindustrial economy requires new skills for collaborative work in reengineered organizations and multiplex networks, our postindustrial democracy requires us to modernize civic skills, institutional capacities, and democratic policy design for a much more complex and diverse public world than existed a half-century ago. And we will need to refashion robust identities of "we, as citizens" capable of engaging in complex coproduction and deliberation to build a shared commonwealth, since the old collective identities and solidarities that underlay previously shared understandings of common interest and public goods during much of the twentieth century have progressively eroded in the wake of underlying structural changes.

Why a Movement?

B ut why do we need a broad civic renewal *movement?* Should we not just concentrate on innovation in specific communities, institutions, and policy arenas?

An expansive movement promises to do several things that innovation in specific arenas alone cannot. Here we focus on the potential of a movement to generate creative new linkages among types of organizations and arenas that are valuable to the work in each; map a wider variety of civic career pathways and avenues for leadership development; and develop a powerful vision to elicit sustained commitment and generate the moral leverage and cultural authority to compel institutional elites to change their usual ways of doing business.

Creative New Partnerships

Thinking in terms of a broad civic renewal movement expands the imagination of the range of potential partners that any given organization might enlist in its work. Movement identities become markers for potential partners, and a common terminology lowers barriers to communication and collaboration. Of course, organizations negotiate on the basis of self-interest, as well as hardheaded calculations about whether investing time and resources in developing new partnerships will pay off. And differences in civic organizing philosophies or organizational turf are not always reconcilable. Yet many differences can be transformed into creative tension, complementarity, and mutual learning. The trend in recent years in virtually all arenas of civic

innovation has been to expand the search for new kinds of
partners to enhance the impact and scope of work. Movement
identities and networks promise to facilitate this further.

Faith-based community organizing, for instance, has selective-
ly expanded its member and partner organizations in recent years
to include unions, universities, community colleges, public
schools, community health centers, and CDCs, as well as
Chambers of Commerce, neighborhood youth groups, immigrant
associations, and environmental organizations. Neighborhood
associations have collaborated with a very broad range of groups,
including watershed associations, CDCs, healthy community
groups, and community policing efforts. As the community
development field opens up to broader "community-building"
approaches, its range of partners in social service and youth
development fields expands considerably. Watershed associations
collaborate with schools, universities, homeowner associations,
fishing and boating clubs, and agricultural and ranching groups,
while environmental justice groups partner with ethnic business
associations, urban gardener groups, and Head Start associations.
As we noted in our discussion of Portland, Oregon, a community
revitalization effort in a specific neighborhood or a restoration
effort in a single watershed might involve dozens or even 100 or
more groups. Engaged campuses increasingly map the widest
array of potential partners with whom their students, along with
faculty and staff, can build long-term, reciprocal relationships
that contribute to both academic learning and community development. Many practitioners in these fields also participate in
"horizontal learning communities" that include agency officials
at every level of the federal system.

Developing such diverse linkages is more than just a matter
of aligning self-interests and strategies. It often requires building
bridges between distinct organizational cultures. In faith-based
organizing, this cultural bridging is facilitated by a common

language of "relationship building," along with core practices such as "one-on-ones." In the community development field, it is abetted by "community assets" terminology and mapping practices, as well as by "community-visioning" and "consensus-building" language and technique. Across these and other fields, such as environmental restoration and community policing, the language of "coproduction" and "cocreation" enables very different kinds of partners to appreciate the meaning and methods of their collaborative public work. In various arenas of planning practice, community dispute resolution, and policy analysis, the common language of "deliberative democracy" helps foster dialogue among disparate groups and interests. And leading practitioners and thinkers in virtually every arena now recognize "social capital" as a core concept.

Not only has the use of such language and practice grown sub-stantially over the past decade, but "multilingual" usage and trans-lation has also increased—a clear sign of the emergence of a broader movement. Thus, organizations whose work crosses various arenas (such as the Center for Democracy and Citizenship) disseminate and interpret the philosophy of "relational organizing" in faith-based community organizing for practitioners and thinkers in other fields. The Kettering Foundation does likewise with such concepts as "deliberative democracy." National practitioner conferences—such as those of the National Network for Youth, Neighborhoods USA, and Campus Compact—include speakers and workshops represent-ing a wide spectrum of approaches. The National Environmental Justice Advisory Council, representing EJ movement leaders and other stakeholders, facilitates translation of ideas and adaptation of models from other arenas of community development and con-sensus building. Best practices manuals, while usually tailored to specific types of work, have grown increasingly ecumenical in inspiration. Thousands of masters degree students in community development, environment, planning, human service, community health, youth development, and public policy programs—who staff many innovative civic projects—have learned these various languages and practices in graduate school (if not earlier) and often in a rich mix that freely intermingles them. Some of the most innovative organizations, such as Alternatives, Inc., and the Hampton Coalition for Youth, are unabashedly multilingual in their efforts to frame and promote youth civic engagement.

Building a broad civic renewal movement will not solve all or even most of the obdurate challenges specific to any given field nor eliminate niche competition. Movement building, however, promises to continue expanding the imagination of potentially productive partnerships and providing the language that enables collaboration. The more richly diverse the types of partners, the more likely that untapped assets will be mobilized and new investments in democracy will be forthcoming.

Expansive Civic Careers

If a movement promises to expand partner relationships spatially, so to speak, it also promises to multiply pathways for the development of civic careers over time. A movement that can enlarge our mental maps of kindred forms of democratic work enables citizens to locate opportunities for continued contributions as they move through the life course, change jobs, relocate to different communities, or shift their issue focus and priorities. A broad movement enables them to envision possible avenues of democratic contribution, whether through their local congregations and communities, their jobs and professions, or their formal political activity and public service. The more citizens can imagine themselves making significant public contributions that fit their other life circumstances, the more likely they are to continue to solidify their civic identities and the less likely they are to lose motivation as a result of substantial gaps in civic activity.

Broad movement networks also increase the opportunities for leadership development over the course of one's civic career. Leaders trained in one arena often seek ways to enhance their skills, broaden their perspectives, and leverage their experiences and networks for larger purpose. The more variegated and progressively challenging are the pathways of leadership development, the more likely that good leaders will be recruited and retained.

We see this already among today's innovative leaders. Thus, an organizer trained by a major faith-based community organizing network later becomes a principal who sparks innovative civic education within his own school and a local network of schools and then comes to direct the national Public Achievement project. By his own account, his relational organizing skills are further refined, his responsibilities enhanced, and his democratic vision and movement map enriched. A community development professional from New York City assumes the executive director's job in a statewide watershed network on the West Coast and spearheads its reinvention around "holistic, community-based, consensus-building strategies," in her words. She sees this work as part of an effort "to reinvent the environmental movement from the ground up" and envisions the watershed movement as part of a larger project to "build social capital" and develop a "new form of citizen governance." A feminist activist, skilled in relational organizing from the women's movement, becomes the director of a citywide office of neighborhood associations. Then, as advisor to the mayor, she helps expand its vision to include other civic associations, new forms of partnership, and a greater focus on equity for poorer communities. A college student gets involved in a national community service network and is then appointed to the board of the Corporation for National Service. She later founds an organization to train young people and adult staff to build youth-adult partnerships but insists that her work makes sense only in terms of a movement for democracy. All four present the specific lessons of their work at various national meetings on civic renewal.

An expansive map of opportunities is especially important for young leaders. Too many young people who engage in community service and service learning as high school or college students fail to transition to other forms of community problem solving and political participation after graduation. Often this drop-off in participation has little to do with whether they maintain their core motivation or have acquired some basic civic skills on which to build. Too often, it results from a narrow field of vision and from networks that are too segmented to help them see a wider democratic panorama. As Merita Irby, Thaddeus Ferber, and Karen Pittman argue, action pathways can serve as well-placed stepping stones that enable young people to move from one issue or organization to another in ways that are both challenging and developmentally appropriate. But action pathways are also "visions into the future, providing direction, hope, achievable dreams, and inspiring action." A key advantage of a broad civic renewal movement is its capacity to expand that democratic vista.

Powerful Democratic Vision

A compelling vision of a vital and dynamic democracy capable of engaging its citizens in work of noble purpose and great consequence is another advantage of a broad movement. Movements with an expansive vision can elicit great moral energy and forge new civic identities. Such movements cannot only help redistribute power, but can also help change values at a much deeper level, one that reverberates throughout many areas of everyday life and institutional practice, as have the civil rights, women's, and environmental movements of previous decades. Movements can generate a sense of efficacy and provide a "grammar of motives" to inspire and sustain commitment. They can provide the moral leverage and cultural authority to compel institutional elites to alter their usual ways of doing business.

While there exist many other strategic and political levels on which movements operate, their capacity to refashion cognitive frames, civic identities, and moral values is now recognized by social movement theorists as among their most important advantages.

Movements with a vision provide the most powerful countervailing forces available to societal actors today. If democracy is threatened by profound cultural and institutional forces, as many studies argue, then we will need a movement with a vision to revitalize democracy in order to address the problem from many different directions simultaneously and meet the challenges in a vigorous and sustained fashion over many years. Without such a movement, there is danger that innovation in any given arena or association will remain segmented, relatively invisible to the public at large, and unable to inspire action on a large enough scale.

In our interviews and strategy conferences with hundreds of civic innovators and young leaders, the view that we need a movement with an expansive vision to revitalize democracy was widely articulated (though by no means fully shared), as was the belief that we need to bring the various networks from different arenas into more productive relationships with each other. When Elizabeth Hollander of Campus Compact said at a strategy conference on higher education, "Don't think small. The future of our democracy is at stake," her view was met with general agreement among leading practitioners and students. A leading innovator with two major national networks in the youth development field, whom we had previously heard speak only in secular terms, said at another strategy conference that civic democracy was "God's vision for the world" and that it was our responsibility to "connect the networks . . . connect the dots" into a larger movement. But perhaps the most poignant testimony came from a middle-school girl engaged in a civic action project that challenged her to think about the "big ideas of democracy." As she put it, "I feel I am writing my signature on the world."

Civic Renewal as a
Movement Master Frame

D eveloping a civic renewal frame is one way that movement thinkers and leaders have begun to connect the dots. Collective action frames are, according to social movement theorists David Snow and Robert Benford, "emergent, action-oriented sets of beliefs and meanings that inspire and legitimate social movement activities and campaigns." Some collective action frames are relatively restricted to specific domains, while others can be elaborated to address a broad range of problems. The civil rights "master frame" exemplifies such elaboration because its core principles of equal rights and opportunities, regardless of ascribed characteristics, could be extended from African American struggles to women's, disability, Native American, student, gay and lesbian, and other rights movements. There are only a limited number of such elaborated movement frames, and the civic renewal frame has developed to the point where it now qualifies as one of these.

Movement framing is an active process that typically entails much debate and disagreement among contributing thinkers, key leaders, and organizations within different niches of the larger field of action. While substantial agreement on core components and metaphors emerges over time, complete consensus or consistency in terms of diagnosis or remedy is never reached and debate often remains quite lively. The civic renewal frame is no different, as we shall see, and some of the disagreement reflects actors' differing relationships to other kinds of movements and to prevailing liberal, progressive, or conservative ideologies.

Movement thinkers draw on three basic sources in developing the civic renewal master frame. First, they engage in frame bridging across civic movements in different arenas. In other words, they build on the reframing work already occurring in fields such as community youth development and civic environmentalism and then tease out the commonalities and the broader significance of practices already in use. And leaders in various movements do much of this bridging already. The community forestry movement and grassroots ecosystem management movement, for instance, borrow core ideas and practices from assets-based community development. The environmental justice movement, though originating with a frame drawn largely from rights and justice movements, has recently added a paradigm-shifting "EJ collaborative problem-solving model" as a result of a conscious search for framing ideas in other civic arenas. This search is driven by bumping up against other practices in ground-level community work and by the limits of the EJ movement's initial framing and practice to achieve adequate results. Because so much frame bridging occurs, the key components of the civic renewal frame we discuss below will already be quite familiar from our discussion in Part One.

Keep in mind, however, that arena-specific reframing also draws on the civic renewal master frame in a reciprocal process. Key framing documents and movement-building initiatives in higher education and K–12 civic education, for instance, have drawn directly on the larger civic renewal frame and networks, and civic environmentalism made a decided shift when its leading thinkers began to address larger questions of civic democracy. The Family Life First movement has been directly inspired by civic renewal framing, and the public journalism movement gained direction and momentum when its innovators entered into dialogue with leaders of the civic renewal movement.

Second, movement thinkers have drawn on the fecund
debates in democratic theory over the past several decades, as
well as on historical reinterpretations of democratic traditions.
Especially important has been theoretical work on deliberative
democracy, civil society, democratic pragmatism, communitarian-
ism, and social capital, plus analytic work on democratic policy
design, regulatory communities, and social trust. Harry Boyte's
renewal of the "democratic commonwealth" tradition in U.S.
history has been particularly fruitful. The third source, especially
important for diagnostic framing, is the broad array of empirical
analyses of the symptoms and causes of civic decline or democratic crisis.

Diagnoses of civic decline, as already noted, vary widely.
Some analysts stress long-term cultural and generational shifts,
while others focus on changes in associational structures and
modes of advocacy and interest group representation. Some
argue that service bureaucracies turn citizens into clients, while
others express concern that such explanations might undermine
support for needed programs. Some point a finger at command-
and-control regulation, while others fear that such reproaches
could help undo needed controls on corporate actors. Some analysts focus on the retreat from civic organizations, while others
worry more about the disengagement from voting and political
campaigns (at least before the 2004 election). Some blame the
escalation of rights without attendant responsibilities, while others view a strong rights orientation as essential to empowering
citizens. Some attend to declining involvement in all types of
communities, while others focus mainly on those that are most
disadvantaged and disenfranchised.

While these and other diagnostic *framing disputes* have
generally been productive, they are unlikely to be resolved to
everyone's satisfaction. But in noting the disagreements, we must
not lose sight of the forest for the trees. The very fact that such

debates have been so intense and sustained for more than a decade and have received considerable attention in civic journals and mass media has opened the space for innovative practitioners to see their work in larger terms and to legitimate it as part of a national project to renew democracy. In addition, intense diagnosis has spurred vigorous calls to action (*motivational framing*) and sustained attention to possible solutions (*prognostic framing*).

A considerable degree of consensus has emerged on the core motivational and prognostic components of the civic renewal master frame, though there are certainly different emphases and framing contests here as well. As we noted in the Introduction, some would stress "service" and "volunteerism" over "coproduction" and "civic professionalism." Others would configure "democracy" and "social justice" or "civil society-state-market" differently from the way we would. Dynamic framing has plenty of room for these kinds of ongoing debates. The clusters of components we see as most central are the following:

Coproducing Public Goods

Producing public goods is a *generalized role of ordinary citizens,* not just a specialized role of public officials. Because public goods are complex, "we, as citizens" must directly contribute to producing them and indeed to defining them. Ordinary citizens—including young people and adults without formal citizenship status—can make substantial contributions and add genuine public value, especially as coproducers acting in concert with professionals and experts. Democracy is, in some fundamental sense, the shared work of citizens acting pragmatically to solve public problems and to build a commonwealth. Citizens who see themselves as cocreators of public goods, rather than simply consumers, are more likely to take ownership of problems and solutions and to invest in developing the requisite civic skills needed to be effective producers. The more that we engage citizens as coproducers, the more that democracy becomes a "way of life," rather than just a form of government.

Thus, public safety is created when neighborhood residents and community organizations coproduce with police, both in defining problems and generating solutions, some of which they implement through self-help efforts. Ecosystems are protected when school science classes develop data bases on river health, watershed associations restore native species, farmers practice sustainable agriculture, boaters monitor illegal dumping, and agency officials and scientists work on stream teams with all these stakeholders to develop coordinated, context-specific knowledge and strategy. Schools become more effective when parents work with teachers and administrators in producing a culture of learning and support and adults enable students to be active learners in the classroom and the community, where they also coproduce goods of visible public value, such as a community playground, restored stream, or citywide bikeways system. Communities become healthier when medical professionals collaborate with civic associations, schools, and churches in promoting healthy lifestyles and building on local knowledge and "citizen science" to reduce environmental hazards.

Central to the idea of citizens as coproducers are two other core concepts in the civic renewal master frame: *community asset mobilization* and *civic professionalism.* All communities have assets that can be mobilized for productive work and visible improvement *if civic actors can shift their mind-set away from deficits and dependence.* In the words of Kretzmann and McKnight's *Building Communities from the Inside Out,* a formative manual used widely across many arenas of civic innovation, "Clients have deficiencies and needs. Citizens have capacities and gifts." Communities typically have unrecognized and underutilized skills and local sources of knowledge. They have civic associations, businesses, and public spaces and institutions of many kinds whose resources and relationships can be mobilized in fresh ways to tackle problems. Such assets can be mapped by ordinary civic actors starting from virtually any organizational or institutional location. Assets-focused strategies do not minimize the role of larger socioeconomic and political forces or the need for external resources. But they prompt citizens to define problems in their own terms, uncover new sources of local investment and creativity, and provide a foundation for hope that elicits new civic energy.

Civic professionalism means that experts reinvent their professional practices—and, indeed, their professional identities—to enable them to coproduce with ordinary citizens and a broad range of stakeholders. It authorizes them to act as citizens in their professional roles and to use their special expertise, but as a *shared resource* rather than as a privileged claim to authority. It means that professionals act as citizens not only outside their formal jobs (as important as this is in providing leadership in the communities and associations of which they are members), but also in making civic practice a core component of their professional practice wherever this might be needed to ensure that their work delivers real public value. Of course, civic professionalism does not entail reinventing all aspects of professional practice and in no way implies that expertise be abdicated. But it does require that professionals continually reflect on how to enable a vital public discourse rather than a narrow technical one, how to recognize and build on local knowledge, and how to ensure civic ownership of problems and broad legitimacy for proposed solutions. And it requires constant alertness to the danger that professional practice can too easily transform citizens into dependent clients and passive spectators and thus fundamentally erode the habits and skills of a self-governing people.

In raising the salience of the citizen as coproducer, the civic renewal frame indicates the limits of other ways in which people typically understand their citizen identities, while recognizing that these also play essential roles in a democracy. Thus, *voters* exercise their rights and fulfill their obligations once every few years and perhaps make serious efforts to stay informed in the interim. Yet their engagement does not necessarily extend further, as they wait to give thumbs up or down to candidates and referenda that offer them periodic choices in the political marketplace. *Taxpayers* provide resources for public programs through their hard-earned income, but the connection of their work to producing public goods ends there, as they wait to pass judgment on officials who put those resources to good or bad, efficient or inefficient uses. *Clients* receive needed social services but too often in asymmetrical relations that breed dependence. *Consumers* of services in the reinvented government marketplace are promised expanded choice and improved quality but have no concomitant responsibilities to make those services work. *Protesters* have been critical to restraining elite power and winning essential rights of recognition for groups previously excluded. But they often moralize conflict in a way that projects all blame for problems onto evil oppressors and leaves little room for pragmatic work with their opponents.

By elaborating the citizen role of coproducer and raising its salience relative to these other typical citizen identities, the civic renewal movement hopes to enhance some of their essential meanings in a fresh admixture. Thus, voters may become more engaged and knowledgeable to the extent that they are generating vital information and doing some policy analysis and public work themselves, as in many watershed and ecosystem restoration projects. Clients can bring new civic energy to communities as programs *enable and expect* them to map and mobilize assets, as in the Comprehensive Community Revitalization Program in the South Bronx. And taxpayers may view their fiscal contributions differently if they see how government can enable citizens like themselves to add further public value. For example, in Seattle's matching grant and community planning programs, citizens voted in favor of more than 470 million dollars in new bonds and levies to fund their proposed projects for libraries, parks, open space, transportation, and low-income housing.

Forging Collaboration out of Conflict

A second core component of the civic renewal master frame is forging collaboration out of conflict. Public life often becomes very contentious as a result of different interests, scarce resources, and unequal power. Such conflict is inevitable and often has been the only way that some groups have been able to achieve basic political recognition and a fairer share of power and resources. Pluralist democracy has developed rules and procedures for representing different interests and managing conflict, but these often prove inadequate in terms of discovering a larger public good and developing more productive solutions to problems. To move forward on various fronts, according to the civic renewal frame, it becomes necessary to develop new forms of collaboration not only among like-minded groups, but also among those with quite different interests, including some previously locked in struggle.

Collaboration is facilitated by a conception of power that is relational rather than zero-sum. The civic renewal frame stresses power as the capacity to act and build relationships. It is "power with" and not "power over," interactive rather than unidirectional. Such power manifests itself, for instance, when faith-based community organizations leverage their capacity to mobilize protests for the purpose of bringing business, political, and educational leaders to the table to develop a collaborative strategy for job training and then follow through on building cross-institutional relationships that will be critical to implementation. Such power operates in a grassroots ecosystem management partnership when environmentalists, farmers, timber companies, and government agencies work together to develop sustainable management practices and restore watersheds, while holding each other accountable through continuous monitoring of results.

Parties with different interests can forge collaboration in various ways. Sometimes they engage in long-term visioning, which enables them to fashion a common picture of what they would like the community to look like in the future and which helps reconfigure how they think of their own interests in relation to the interests of others— "self-interest rightly understood," in Tocqueville's famous phrase. Sometimes they choose to work on limited projects in which their interests are less polarized and, after building trust and seeing results, move on to more contentious issues. Sometimes they use very structured consensus-building techniques. But the specific set of techniques for dialogue and deliberation are less important than the general belief that parties with very diverse and sometimes conflicting interests can forge new bases of trust, hold each other accountable for concrete results, and alter the way they view their self-interests.

The civic renewal master frame does *not* hold that *all* conflict can be transformed in this way, that *all* power is relational, or that interest group representation, advocacy, and resistance lose all relevance. Indeed, to forge collaboration, strong countervailing power and capacity to impose costs through protest or legal action often become necessary. But the frame does hold that there is far greater opportunity to transform conflict into productive collaboration than our usual ways of doing politics allow. And it holds that, to move forward as a society in the present era, we need to make relational power strategies much more central to how we carry out our public affairs.

Robust Civil Society, Catalytic Government, Embedded Market

A third component of the civic renewal master frame is a reconfigured balance between government, market, and civil society that transforms each in the interests of greater self-government, coproduction, and collaboration.

A robust civil society, in the civic renewal frame, includes a variety of civic associations that engage in mutual aid and problem solving and develop the arts of democratic leadership and self-governance on a broad scale. While many civic associations quite naturally focus on local neighborhood, common faith, ethnic identity, or other bases of social similarity, civil society in an inclusive, pluralist democracy of the twenty-first century must generate many new bridges across old boundaries. In the words of John Gardner, who contributed substantially to developing this frame in the last decade of his life, civic renewal recognizes a "pluralistic web of communities," connected externally through links to the city, region, nation, global economy, and biosphere and internally through relationships among families, neighbors, associations, local institutions, and businesses. Revitalizing democracy, as well as building requisite capacities for problem solving across a wide range of issues, depends on "reweaving the fabric" of communities and civil society, to use another common metaphor.

Thus, faith-based community organizing builds a more robust civil society because it reaches across old boundaries of religious denomination, race, ethnicity, and city/suburb and because it builds trust among parties with different interests (and sometimes conflicts) in a pragmatic search for workable partnerships. Neighborhood associations in well-designed citywide systems collaborate with other civic, environmental, and educational organizations and are encouraged to develop local land use and other plans with an eye to surrounding neighborhoods and diverse voices within their own. In some cases, they operate within regional or statewide growth management laws and strategies. An ecosystem partnership might mobilize assets and recruit leadership through a broad range of farming and ranching associations, environmental organizations and outdoors groups, churches, and 4-H clubs—all in the name of a sustainable regional economy and ecosystem and within the bounds of state and federal environmental laws.

Catalytic government, in the civic renewal frame, facilitates citizen problem solving and serves as a partner in multisided collaborative efforts. It is government as a civic catalyst, a provider of tools and resources to aid citizens in their work. In the phrase of a prominent innovator and interagency organizer within the federal government for the past three decades who contributed directly to the civic renewal frame, it is government that "puts the 'civil' back in civil service." This entails rethinking the role of public administrators as one of strengthening the capacities and responsibilities of citizens and dispersing initiative downward and outward, wherever possible, while establishing inclusive democratic criteria for participation. It also means convening stakeholders from civic associations and businesses to facilitate more productive deliberation, trust, and collaboration. Although the civic renewal movement is decidedly shaped by critiques of social service bureaucracies that foster one-way dependence and ensnare citizens in a maze of categorical programs, as well as by critiques of regulatory bureaucracies that rely disproportionately on command-and-control, its master frame rejects antagonism to the federal government as either service provider or regulator. It seeks instead to restore trust in national public institutions by linking service and regulatory functions much more closely to building capacities for community problem solving and by investing substantial public resources to accomplish this.

Thus, the police and school departments in Chicago invest resources to enable police officers, principals, and teachers to work with parents and local residents in developing strategies for school improvement and crime reduction. These agencies also hold them all accountable for effective deliberation and substantive progress—a design for "accountable autonomy," in Archon Fung's apt phrase. Federal and state environmental officials can invest resources that enable local stakeholders to collaborate in ecosystem management—and help form new associations on a wide scale—while ensuring that the goals of national environmental laws are fulfilled, or even surpassed. The Office of University Partnerships at HUD and Learn and Serve at the Corporation for National and Community Service can provide resources to build the capacity of a wide range of educational associations, which in turn help schools and universities develop effective service-learning programs and community-university partnerships.

An *embedded market,* in the civic renewal frame, is one in which business actors make decisions informed and constrained by the broader set of social relationships in which their corporate entities are embedded. In this frame, business leaders contribute to multistakeholder problem solving rather than impose their will unilaterally on communities and workers. They engage in visioning with a broad range of citizens and civic associations and open themselves to deliberation about broad values, rather than just narrow profit calculations. When business leaders find some government regulations counterproductive, they opt to participate in democratic regulatory communities capable of multisided learn-ing with agency officials and empowered citizen groups, instead of campaigning for outright deregulation. They empower employees to reengineer their work to support broad public goals and limit negative externalities, such as environmental harm, and they work collaboratively with unions and professional associations on redesign. They respond to employee needs for alternative working time arrangements—such as flextime, job sharing, and part-time professional work—to enable them to be responsible parents and engaged community members. Executives recognize community service and engagement as important components of corporate culture and provide tangible supports and incentives for these. And they explore how to use the workplace as a forum for civic discussion and education. In these and other ways, good corporate citizenship—and the "corporate citizenship movement"—can become essential components of broad civic renewal.

Of course, this configuration of robust civil society, catalytic government, and embedded market can take many different forms, and there invariably will be disagreement—political and scholarly—over which works best. The civic renewal master frame insists, however, that in deciding the most appropriate configuration for a specific community, type of market, public good, or regulatory challenge, we focus on how our design choices will enhance or inhibit capacities for citizen self-government and coproduction.

Rights and Justice in the Civic Renewal Frame

The civic renewal master frame is primarily a *pragmatic democracy frame* in which "we, as citizens" are producers and problem solvers with the skills and power to generate effective collaboration amidst differing and often conflicting interests. This distinguishes it from most rights and justice frames of social movements in recent decades. Rights movements have focused on basic claims to social and political recognition and inclusion, and social justice movements have stressed the redistribution of power and resources. The civic renewal movement certainly builds on myriad achievements of these movements; many of its leading thinkers and practitioners have activist histories within rights and justice movements. But, through the lens of the civic renewal frame, the conceptions of democracy in these other movements are not robust enough to secure effective self-government in an increasingly complex and diverse society. *Recognition and redistribution, alone or in combination, prove inadequate without coproduction—that is, without a much more profound sense of the productive side of everyday politics than rights and justice movements typically provide.* The civic renewal movement does not aspire to displace rights and justice movements, which serve a variety of legitimate and distinct purposes. But it does seek to enrich the mix of democratic ideas and models for fashioning a more inclusive and just society.

Innovative civic groups configure civic renewal, social justice, and civil rights in diverse ways. This diversity depends partly on the kinds of institutional settings in which they work, as well as the other movements with which they intersect. Thus, at one end of the spectrum lies the environmental justice movement, whose dominant frame has been a strong blend of social justice and civil rights, reflecting the influence of other movements as well as the intensity of local fears and confrontations over toxic threats. However, as grassroots environmental justice organizations learn to work with other institutions in the community development field and receive support for community-based remedies from government agencies, their frame shifts considerably toward the "EJ collaborative problem-solving model." Faith-based community organizing employs a social justice frame rooted in the religious traditions of its member congregations. But its key precept of working on issues that unite rather than divide poor and working-class communities restrains the proliferation of rights claims by distinctly aggrieved groups. Its ideal of "ethical democracy" and strategy of building sustainable relationships with powerful institutions and sometime adversaries, such as banks, businesses, and school systems, preempts tendencies toward constructing adversarial identities ("us versus them," "victim versus oppressor," "good versus evil") common in social justice movements. Civic renewal groups tend to resist such dichotomies and refuse to attribute blame for public problems to one side alone.

At the other end of the spectrum, one finds the service-learning movement and other initiatives to renew the civic mission of K–12 schools. Here the civic renewal frame is ascendant (competing primarily with "service") because democracy has long been a core value of schooling. In addition, public schools are constrained from taking substantive rights and justice positions that might be overly contentious in local communities or might interfere with public and professional norms of learning from multiple perspectives. Furthermore, civic education policy change often requires support from political actors who differ considerably on a range of substantive rights and justice issues. Yet many classes and extracurricular groups engage in projects with rights and justice themes, and in private or religious schools with strong social justice traditions, this may be the dominant orientation of service learning and related activities. The movement to renew the civic mission of higher education has a very strongly articulated civic renewal frame for many of the same reasons K–12 education does. However, many service-learning courses provide opportunities to work on rights and social justice issues, and some private (especially religious) colleges, as well as a few public universities, define their overall civic education approach in terms of social justice. The civic journalism frame is unambiguously a democracy frame because of professional norms that favor open debate and constrain substantive positions on social justice issues in the main reporting sections of mainstream commercial and public news media. The information commons movement includes a panoply of institutional actors, such as libraries and universities, that inform its democratic commonwealth frame, even as it raises many issues of equity and justice in access to information.

Of course, many other variations exist both within and among different arenas. Neighborhood associations, community visioning, study circles, and community policing are founded upon inclusive rights to participate and are relatively open to civic actors raising questions of social justice. They also enable citizens to do work that improves the lives of those least well off.

But they are not defined *primarily* as rights or social justice models. Civic environmental projects for open land protection often incorporate affordable housing as a social justice issue. Community youth development includes groups that primarily use a civic renewal frame, as well as those that include social justice as an essential, if not dominant, component. Even within a single organization we often find variation. The YMCA of the USA, for instance, uses a civic renewal frame in its civic engagement initiatives, yet some local Y's define their main service learning as social or environmental justice.

The civic renewal master frame *foregrounds pragmatic democracy* because it sees democracy in the United States as endangered from many directions and because it recognizes an increasing number of public problems that cannot be addressed adequately unless citizens develop new methods of coproduction and collaboration. Such framing, it is believed, opens up new sources of civic energy and effectiveness *that would otherwise remain unavailable* if the typical array of rights and justice frames were the primary ones used in diagnosing problems, motivating action, and imagining solutions. Like other frames, the civic renewal frame seeks to establish its credibility through empirical evidence (such as new resources brought to the table to solve problems and high satisfaction with results from previously marginalized racial and ethnic groups), as well as through congruence with scientific and professional paradigms (such as what factors produce health and public safety or how ecosystems work).

In the complex mix of what many analysts now call our social movement society, civic actors often stand in the crosscurrents of various movements simultaneously, and they creatively commingle and recombine ideas and models from each. While the civic renewal movement does not aspire to displace rights and justice movements, it does seek to enrich their democratic frames and practices and in some cases to help reinvent them, just as, for example, civic environmentalism seeks to (partially) reinvent the environmental movement. But the civic renewal movement must also recognize that these other movements will, in turn, challenge the civic renewal frame to respond to their core concerns. There is already significant complementarity and mutual learning, both at the grassroots level and among the leadership of these various movements, and much opportunity to make remaining tensions progressively more productive over time.

Over the past decade, the civic renewal movement has emerged from the efforts of innovators who have not only reworked basic paradigms and promoted best practices in specific arenas, but who have also contributed to a larger movement master frame and forged networks across various civic movements. These innovators have engaged in a number of ambitious movement-building projects and established important foundations for growth in the coming years.

Nonetheless, the civic renewal movement is far from having become a robust and recognized movement in American society. In this section, we examine several movement-building projects, as well as specific impediments to the further development of the movement. Some obstacles are inherent in a movement that is not primarily a rights or justice movement and thus cannot draw on the familiar tactical repertoire of sit-ins, freedom rides, and boycotts. Other difficulties derive from the breadth of the movement's democratic frame, which addresses an epochal "challenge"—even generalized "crisis"—of civic democracy deriving from multiple sources and thus attempts to elicit collaboration from a correspondingly wide array of organizational actors and networks. Many organizations, however, already find their resources stretched thin in their respective arenas, whether this be faith-based community organizing, community youth development, or ecosystem restoration. They may, therefore, be skeptical of making significant investments in broader movement building and may have quite varied or ill-formed views of what such a movement would look like. Still other challenges involve what social movement theorists call "political opportunity structures" that open up yet also delimit chances to gain public visibility and political support.

In light of these obstacles to building a broad renewal movement that links various innovative civic projects and other movements, it is wise to proceed with cautious realism without abandoning a wider vision of a revitalized democracy. If the movement is to continue to grow, it will be through methodical work that further develops relationships across networks. Without a significant infusion of foundation funding and new political and policy opportunities, movement building is likely to be a slow process—and one in danger of stalling. And movement building must, first and foremost, respect the constraints posed by work in each specific arena.

Nonetheless, we expect to continue to see ambitious projects and bold proposals with interrelated parts that take seriously the fact that the democratic "challenge" or "crisis" of our era is not a problem of segmented arenas such as civic education, community development, or electoral reform but one that impacts our civic culture and institutions broadly. Movements, of course, not only seize new political opportunities but also help create them.

Movement-Building Initiatives

A number of movement-building initiatives have been undertaken in the past decade to develop the civic renewal frame, publicize best practices, broaden networks, and shape public discourse. These projects have been moderately successful in establishing a foundation for the movement, though one that will have to be strengthened considerably if the movement is to continue to grow. Here we look briefly at four initiatives, although other projects have also contributed in various ways. The four are the Reinventing Citizenship Project and American Civic Forum; the Alliance for National Renewal; the National Commission on Civic Renewal; and the Saguaro Seminar.

Reinventing Citizenship Project and American Civic Forum

Directed by Harry Boyte of the Center for Democracy and Citizenship at the University of Minnesota and funded by the Ford Foundation, the Reinventing Citizenship Project and the American Civic Forum in 1994 brought together several core partners (Project Public Life, the Kettering Foundation, the Progressive Policy Institute, and the Walt Whitman Center at Rutgers University) with a variety of other civic networks engaged in innovation, as well as various innovators in federal agencies, National Public Radio, and the Public Broadcasting System. Reinventing Citizenship convened civic innovators and federal officials under the auspices of William Galston, deputy assistant for domestic policy in the Clinton administration, to explore the ways in which government might serve as a catalyst for civic problem solving and the "reinventing government" initiative (under Vice President Al Gore) might develop more robust civic components. The American Civic Forum emerged out of this when practitioners from various arenas called for an ongoing network of organizations to promote the general themes and best practices of civic renewal.

These projects accomplished several important tasks. First, they began a broad inventory of models of civic innovation in a variety of arenas and established some core commonalties. Second, they brought innovators from various arenas into dialogue and established that many, including some who knew little of innovation in arenas outside their own, wanted to see their work as part of a larger movement to renew democracy in the United States. Third, these projects developed key components of the civic renewal frame, especially in drafting the *Civic Declaration: A Call for a New Citizenship,* which was circulated widely and, along with related documents, helped in reframing the role of civic engagement in several arenas, such as higher education, youth development, public journalism, and civic education. Fourth, these projects garnered important media attention that (along with the Alliance for National Renewal, which we discuss below) led a number of prominent syndicated columnists to begin speaking of the new "citizenship movement." And, finally, the emerging "civil society" and "civic renewal" themes of some politicians, most notably Senator Bill Bradley, were directly shaped by the participation of several aides and advisors in these projects.

Without further foundation funding, Reinventing Citizenship and the American Civic Forum were unable to sustain themselves. Yet they spawned two other projects that further contributed to the development of the movement. In 1995, the Civic Practices Network (www.cpn.org), a partnership among various national civic organizations and university centers, emerged as the earliest of the Web sites promoting the general civic renewal frame along with important reframing documents in specific arenas. CPN's core partners included the Center for Youth and Communities (Brandeis University), School of Journalism and Mass Communication (University of Wisconsin-Madison), Center for Democracy and Citizenship (University of Minnesota), National Civic League, Kettering Foundation, Study Circles Resources Center, Alliance for National Renewal, and Pew Center for Civic Journalism. Other organizations who contributed in various ways include the League of Women Voters Education Fund, Wisconsin Public Television, Public Broadcasting System, International Youth Foundation, American Health Decisions, Common Enterprise, Walt Whitman Center (Rutgers University), Project on Public Life and the Press (New York University), Hastings Center for Bioethics, Pew Partnership for Civic Change, and Computer Professionals for Social Responsibility. CPN has also provided extensive case studies drawn from scholars and practitioners, as well as a variety of best-practices manuals. Its case studies and field-mapping essays have been used by all subsequent movement-building projects. In the early days of the World Wide Web, CPN disseminated Web-based manuals of best practices even of prominent national organizations not yet capable of doing so themselves and also provided the first home pages for various innovative civic organizations, such as the Dudley Street Neighborhood Initiative and Oregon Health Decisions.

The second initiative to emerge from the Reinventing Citizenship Project and American Civic Forum was the National Commission on Civic Renewal, to which we return below.

The Alliance for National Renewal

In 1994, proceeding largely on a separate track, the National Civic League (NCL) celebrated its one hundredth anniversary with a project designed to build a broad civic renewal movement.

Under John Parr's leadership, NCL had been an important movement entrepreneur for nearly a decade with its work on community visioning, healthy communities, and other innovative civic strategies built around the use of its *Civic Index*, including its well-publicized annual All-America City Awards conference. John Gardner, chair of the NCL board, had spent much of 1992 surveying innovative community-building efforts around the country and had become convinced that such a movement was both necessary and already emergent. Gardner, legendary founder of Common Cause, Independent Sector, and other important citizen advocacy organizations, as well as a widely read author on leadership, drew on his extensive networks in the nonprofit sector, as did others on the NCL staff and board who had been active in innovative regional planning, public/private partnerships, and local reinventing government efforts.

The Alliance for National Renewal (ANR) was formally launched in late 1994 at the annual NCL Conference on Governance with representatives from 40 organizations. Under the guidance of NCL President Chris Gates and former Vice President Gloria Rubio-Cortes, it expanded to include some 230 by the end of the decade. Over this period, ANR accomplished several important tasks. First, it further helped diffuse the civic renewal frame through conferences and publications. Gardner's booklet, *National Renewal,* sold more than 100,000 copies, primarily through ANR networks, and was also widely distributed by CPN over the Internet. Second, ANR brought many organizations into relationship with one another and familiarized them with innovative civic practices. National organizations, such as United Way of America and Independent Sector, were aided in promoting community-building approaches through clusters of local innovators in their own affiliated chapters and networks. Professional organizations, such as the American Planning Association, National Institute of Dispute Resolution, International City/County Association,

Council on Excellence in Government, Alliance for Redesigning Government, National League of Cities, and National Academy of Public Administration, found further networks and tools to refine the civic dimensions of their work. Third, ANR garnered additional media attention, which raised the visibility of the movement. Fourth, the especially well developed links of ANR and NCL to local political leaders further promoted the language and practice of civic problem solving, as did former Senator Bill Bradley at the national level when he assumed the role of NCL board chair after Gardner stepped down.

Despite these important achievements, ANR was not able to sustain itself as a separate network beyond 2002, though the National Civic League still performs some of ANR's functions.

The National Commission on Civic Renewal

Through the efforts of William Galston and the Reinventing Citizenship Project, the Clinton administration decided to make civic renewal a centerpiece of the 1995 State of the Union Address. As a *Newsweek* headline put it, "Clinton's State of the Union could be a blueprint for the next big theme in politics—reinventing citizenship—if he can follow it." But he didn't, and as a result, two important proposals were abandoned. One proposal was for a White House office ("civic partnership council") designed to propagate innovative civic models throughout the federal government and to lay the basis for a much richer public discourse on the importance of civic engagement in community and institutional renewal. The other called for a Presidential Commission on Reinventing Citizenship. When Galston left the White House, however, he secured funding for a national commission from the Pew Charitable Trusts, whose newly appointed director of the Public Policy Program, Paul Light, had been a key participant in Reinventing Citizenship.

The National Commission on Civic Renewal, directed by Galston and Deputy Director Peter Levine, convened four plenary sessions during 1997–1998. Its contributions included the first sustained and highly visible discussion among nationally prominent liberals and conservatives on the fundamentals of civic renewal. Cochaired by Sam Nunn, former Democratic senator from Georgia, and William Bennett, former secretary of education under President Reagan, the commission heard testimony from leading thinkers across the political spectrum on important questions, such as the role of government, neighborhoods, media, family, and education in a vital civic democracy. It also commissioned a series of scholarly papers to guide deliberation and brought further focus on best practices in a number of arenas. Because of its composition, the commission was able to garner substantial media coverage for the problem. Second, the commission's senior advisory council included a dozen individuals prominent in the civic renewal movement, and the commission's final report, *A Nation of Spectators,* further developed the frame and validated the identity of the movement. Third, the commission developed an index of national civic health that further reinforced the diagnostic frame of crisis. And, finally, the commission's recommendation for a civic education initiative led to the development of the National Alliance for Civic Education and eventually to the formation of CIRCLE and the strategy built around *The Civic Mission of Schools.*

The Saguaro Seminar: Civic Engagement in America

Convened by Robert Putnam of the Kennedy School of Government at Harvard and cochaired by Chris Gates (from NCL, ANR, CPN, and the National Commission on Civic Renewal), the Saguaro Seminar brought together several leaders who had participated in these other projects, innovators from youth development and other arenas, as well as a group of scholars, journalists, and former elected officials and key Democratic and Republican political advisors. In eight meetings between 1997 and 2000, participants explored the relation of social capital to government, arts, technology, religion, work, and youth. They helped further deepen the analysis of social capital in Putnam's landmark book, *Bowling Alone* (2000), and guided the case selections for a subsequent book, *Better Together: Restoring the American Community* (2003), which focused still further attention on the upside of civic innovation, rather than just the downside of social capital depletion.

The Saguaro Seminar not only raised the visibility of best practices, but its final report, issued in 2000, also set a broad agenda linking reform strategies in each arena studied. It attracted still further media and political attention for civic renewal. And it further validated the idea that a "new period of civic renaissance" requires a "broad grassroots movement to reengage America."

Further Efforts

These four sets of projects, of course, do not represent the full spectrum of efforts to build a civic renewal movement. The Kettering Foundation, an operating and research foundation that focuses on the public and its role in democracy, under the leadership of David Mathews, has not only contributed to several of these projects directly, but also its research and publications have refined the civic renewal frame and spurred innovative work across various arenas, including higher education, public policy deliberation, community dialogue, and public journalism. The Kettering Foundation helped set the stage for the emergence of the movement with publications such as The Harwood Institute's *Main Street* study of citizens and politics in 1991. This study was the subject of more than 1,000 newspaper stories and editorials, including a lead editorial in the *New York Times*, David Broder's syndicated column in 140 newspapers, and Associated Press articles in at least 262. Kettering's work also reverberates throughout a very extensive network of civic and educational organizations, including critical ones in most arenas we have examined.

During the late 1990s, the Center for Living Democracy's American News Service, an ANR partner organization, widely publicized "stories of renewal" through its subscriber network of 300 newspapers, including leading ones such as the *Los Angeles Times, Boston Globe,* and *Christian Science Monitor.* The Harwood Institute and Public Agenda have done important research and polling using a civic frame and have facilitated the work of many other innovative organizations. The Pew Partnership for Civic Change has provided leadership training and research on innovative civic models across a variety of arenas. The Democracy Collaborative, a consortium of 20 university centers and civic organizations hosted by the University of Maryland, promotes democratic and civic renewal locally, nationally, and globally through a variety of projects.

In the late 1990s, several other projects convened civic and political leaders, along with scholars of democracy, to raise the visibility of civic action, community service, and democratic dialogue in tackling public problems. These initiatives included the National Commission on Philanthropy and Civic Renewal (Bradley Foundation); Penn National Commission on Society, Culture, and Community (University of Pennsylvania); America*Speaks;* and the President's Summit for America's Future (now America's Promise). The last, initially led by General Colin Powell as chair and former HUD secretary Henry Cisneros as vice chair, received the support of President Clinton; former presidents Bush, Carter, and Ford; and former First Lady Nancy Reagan. It retains its focus on broad community action to improve the lives of young people. Providing further media visibility for the frame of civic action and dialogue were two yearlong series under the PBS Democracy Project, *Citizens '96* and *Citizens State of the Union.* Wisconsin Public Television produced these series in collaboration with civic journalism partners in ten cities within an overall project design shaped by an advisory board of civic renewal movement leaders linked through the Alliance for National Renewal. A CBS Radio *Osgood File* project on community and democracy and National Public Radio's democracy and citizens' election projects also drew on these networks.

Persistent Challenges

W hile these projects have laid important foundations for the development of the civic renewal movement and while civic innovation has made significant progress over the last decade in most arenas profiled here, movement growth nonetheless faces persistent challenges. On the positive side, the civic renewal frame has developed as a distinctive master frame with relatively robust diagnostic, prognostic, and motivational components and is well positioned to be refined as it grapples with further research, practice, and critique. Its cultural resonance with pragmatic American values of democratic problem solving and community initiative is considerable. The evidentiary basis of innovative civic practice is vastly more developed than it was a decade ago, and various practical tool kits have become more sophisticated and readily available. Networks have been developed across important arena-specific organizations, and some national leaders and organizations have collaborated on multiple projects. Local civic partnerships have also become more diverse and expansive and are increasingly apt to employ common language, thereby strengthening the relational and ideational basis for a broader movement. There now exists a well-recognized national public discourse on the problem of democracy and civic engagement, as well as some clearly established channels to local and national media. The basic appeal of the rhetoric of active citizen engagement and service has proven itself under both Democratic and Republican administrations.

Nonetheless, the civic renewal movement still has a long way to go to become a robust movement capable of transforming civic

culture, institutional practice, and public policy. Innovation in
each arena confronts major obstacles, ranging from professional
and bureaucratic practices to policy design and power resources
—obstacles that we, unfortunately, cannot explore here.
Movement networks are very unevenly developed across specific
arenas and have major gaps; in most cases they do not extend
deeply into the middle and lower tiers of leadership. While an
increasing number of these leaders are becoming cognizant of the
larger discourse about democracy and social capital, a much
smaller number are aware of the existence of a broad civic renewal movement. Nor do many recognize its purpose, distinct from
the civic movement they might identify with in their own arena
or other rights and social justice movements that they may see as
leveraging their work for larger purpose. The civic renewal movement has not achieved clear recognition in the media or among
the larger public and does not have the leverage to shape policy
design systematically. And while national political leaders have
become more attuned to the rhetoric of civic problem solving
and service, they have not felt compelled by movement activity
to respond in any consistent and substantial manner or to commit
significant public investments to help modernize our civic
infrastructure.

These movement-building problems derive from several
sources.

- *Breadth and diversity.* First, the breadth and manifold
  character of the civic crisis, the relative inclusivity of the
  civic renewal master frame, and the diverse types of actors
  and innovative civic models in various arenas present a
  distinct challenge of focus for movement building. Even
  within specific arenas, different models often compete for
  resources and recognition, and sometimes even for the
  same turf, despite increasing tendencies to use common
  language. Building a movement across arenas runs into
  the further challenge of justifying investments of scarce

time and resources on activities that may seem to have little immediate and direct benefit to arena-specific work. No common advocacy agenda for renewing democracy, at least at this point, motivates broad collaboration. Some important democratic reform agendas, such as campaign finance, electoral reform, and youth voting, tend to become privileged by the media and foundations in a way that can easily crowd out models of innovative civic problem solving and public work.

- *Tactical repertoire.* Second, while the civic renewal movement builds upon many of the democratic achievements of recent movements for civil rights and social justice, it is not a rights or justice movement per se. And because it seeks to foster new forms of civic collaboration and public work among groups that may differ on important issues, it cannot use the repertoire of many recent rights and justice movements nor, for that matter, fundamentalist religious movements. The civic renewal movement cannot inspire action on the basis of unconditional claims to rights or righteous struggles against clearly defined oppressors. It cannot invoke metaphors of unambiguous good and evil or moral resistance in the face of power. It cannot capture and focus public attention through mass protests, marches on Washington, boycotts, strikes, freedom rides, or sit-ins, nor can it count on repression by authorities to galvanize widespread support. The civic renewal movement cannot expect dramatic court decisions (like *Brown v. Board of Education* or *Roe v. Wade)* to energize activists or secure significant new levers of power and representation. It lacks a constitutional amendment (like the Nineteenth Amendment or the failed Equal Rights Amendment) around which to organize. And while legislation could certainly enact policy designs that help build civic capacity in specific arenas, as some of our cases have indicated, a broadly based civic renewal movement cutting across many institutional sectors cannot at this point hope to build its networks through advocacy coalitions or lobbying for specific laws.

• *Political opportunity.* Third, the political structure presents certain opportunities but also serious obstacles to the growth and recognition of the civic renewal movement. Despite supporting much civic and community-based innovation through various federal agency programs and despite its initial support for Reinventing Citizenship, the Clinton administration backed away from larger efforts. Several factors may have influenced this retreat: a) the distractions created by the new Republican majority in Congress in 1994 at exactly the point when Reinventing Citizenship required focus to move forward on several key proposals and related collaborative projects between civic partners and top agency officials; b) a calculation that there was little immediate political gain to be had from the Reinventing Citizenship focus; and c) the preference of some close to Clinton for a left-populist rather than a civic-populist frame, which was also manifest in Gore's "the people vs. the powerful" campaign of 2000.

President George W. Bush also called on Americans "to be citizens, not spectators," and his 2002 State of the Union address, the first after the events of 9/11, reinforced this call with the promise of ambitious national service initiatives. But the administration's efforts to leverage the enhanced spirit of a civic "we" have been hampered by several factors: a) resistance among congressional Republicans to using government to support national service; b) the controversial and relatively narrow focus of the White House Office of Faith-Based and Community Initiatives and concomitant legislation; and c) a frame of "compassionate conservatism" that may not be robust enough to accommodate the range or depth of civic innovation.

In addition, during the first Bush administration, the war on terror tended to crowd out domestic issues, and the war in Iraq generated a degree of political polarization that lessened the immediate resonance of a frame of civic collaboration, at least in organized political circles. And state and local budget shortfalls in the early 2000s, along with the decline in foundation endowments compared with the boom years of the 1990s, has led to programmatic narrowing and cutbacks for many local innovators. For some community organizations at our national strategy conferences in 2001–2002, for instance, "civic democracy" appeared as a luxury in the face of the challenges of "survival."

A fuller analysis of political opportunities and policy options to strengthen and extend civic innovation would take us beyond the bounds of this book and would beg answers to questions that inevitably have partisan implications, which is not our purpose here. Nonetheless, it is important to outline what we see as some of the parameters of partisanship and nonpartisanship in building the civic renewal movement, as well as some ideas within the two major parties that might help create new political opportunities.

Partisanship and Nonpartisanship in the Movement

T he civic renewal movement sees itself largely as a nonpartisan movement, though many of its leading thinkers and practitioners also have partisan identities and commitments. In our view, both partisanship and nonpartisanship have roles to play in defining and building the movement, but it is important to clarify how and where such distinctions should be operative.

First, nonpartisanship is essential for many types of institutions and organizations central to civic renewal. In some, nonpartisanship is mandated by law, as in the case of city offices of neighborhood involvement and planning, city youth commissions, community policing beat meetings, and public school and university programs in civic education and service learning. In others, nonpartisanship is virtually required by institutional missions and diverse boards of directors, such as the YMCA, 4-H, and virtually all private institutions of higher education. In still other cases, nonpartisanship has become a requisite of trust building in multistakeholder partnerships, such as healthy community coalitions and ecosystem restoration partnerships. Such collaborative and mutually accountable work cannot be done with integrity if any important set of stakeholders feels that others are driven by overt or covert partisan agendas. This is also the case for community visioning, study circles, and other forms of deliberative democratic dialogue and consensus building.

In faith-based community organizing, nonpartisanship is a matter of choice determined by the requirements of strategic relationships with changing political administrations, although the increasingly metropolitan character of coalitions (and hence suburban congregations that are members alongside inner-city ones) also makes nonpartisanship a virtual necessity. And for many organizations, nonpartisanship is a prerequisite for public funding, as well as for most private foundation funding.

Second, the practice of civic professionalism, whether in nonprofit, government or market institutions, typically requires nonpartisanship. Certainly all of the local, state, and federal programs that facilitate and support citizen coproduction, in partnership with professionals, are fundamentally nonpartisan. And the more that we recognize administrative and policy design-for-democracy as essential to civic renewal, the more nonpartisan must be any movement that tries to fashion a common frame and shared sense of mission among the many kinds of civic, business, and administrative actors whose collaboration in renewing democracy is essential.

Third, the civic renewal movement is a movement committed to learning openly and self-critically from a pluralistic array of democratic practices and civic models. No single model possesses all the answers or is without its downside. All must be judged in practice and in response to appropriate measures of effectiveness. This self-critical, pluralist, and performance-based ethos runs counter to the normal reflexes of partisan rhetoric and strategic advantage.

However, while nonpartisanship remains central to the movement, civic renewal cannot succeed without supportive public policies and a coherent politics. It thus cannot avoid engagement with the party system. This will require movement leaders to develop principled and effective ways of bridging the worlds of nonpartisan civic engagement and problem solving, on the one hand, and partisan activity, on the other. While it is not our purpose here to analyze the relative merits of various policy

designs or party positions and strategies on civic renewal—nor
to stake out our own partisan stance—it is important to recognize
that, over the past decade, various groupings within the two
major parties have begun to formulate ideas that can expand
political opportunities for the civic renewal movement.

Foremost in developing civic renewal themes within the
Democratic Party has been the Progressive Policy Institute, the
think tank affiliated with the Democratic Leadership Council
(DLC). "The New Progressive Declaration: A Political Philosophy
for the Information Age" draws directly upon the work of two
of its four coauthors, Will Marshall and William Galston, in
various movement-building projects (Reinventing Citizenship,
the American Civic Forum, and the National Commission on
Civic Renewal). As the declaration argues, the New Progressives
constitute "not a party or faction but a broad civic movement
dedicated to radical reform" that seeks "to build new common
ground, not new partisan divisions." A philosophy of civic
empowerment forms the core of the new governing philosophy
in which citizens directly participate in producing public goods
and where "old civic virtues find fresh expression in new democratic institutions and in a new covenant between citizens and
their commonwealth."

The New Progressives offer a third choice between what they
see as the left's reflexive defense of the bureaucratic status quo
and the right's destructive bid to dismantle government. This
path entails transforming government into a "catalyst for a
broader civic enterprise, controlled by and responsive to the
needs of citizens and the communities where they live and
work." The shift to forms of self-government appropriate to the
information age will not occur without a strategy to restore
opportunity by fostering new conditions for citizens to create
wealth through public and private investment, promote worker
access to lifelong learning, and develop innovative ways for

managing and organizing every aspect of work. Nor will it occur, according to the New Progressives, without a serious national debate about corporate accountability and governance in the economy or without fresh efforts to reinvent unions and other forms of worker association to enhance economic power and community self-help in a global information society. Critical to any strategy based on building the capacities of individual citizens and communities for self-governance and the production of wealth is a renewed national commitment to generate for the urban poor economic opportunities based on work, savings, and entrepreneurship.

Other important thinkers of the Democratic Party have also incorporated the theme of civil society into their strategic vision for a populist progressivism capable of addressing the needs of ordinary working individuals and families. Most notably, Stanley Greenberg and Theda Skocpol have accepted the message of moderate Democrats that "civil society must be central to democratic renewal. Along with government at all levels, communities, religious institutions, and businesses must be engaged as partners in a larger quest for the good society." Greenberg and Skocpol criticize the economic populists on the Democratic left who focus primarily on workplace issues of unionized blue-collar workers in large transnational corporations. In contrast, they develop a family-centered agenda to enable working parents to fulfill their civic obligations in raising their children; nurturing civic life in neighborhoods, churches, and schools; and caring for elders. They frame the defense of various entitlement programs, from paid parental leave to Social Security, in these terms. Although they are deeply critical of what they see as the DLC's reflexive tendency to favor markets in various policy arenas, they recognize that a winning progressive strategy that renews civil society will have to learn from the existing Democratic center and left alike—a view shared by other influential thinkers, such as E.J. Dionne.

Civic conservatives within the Republican Party have also addressed the issues of community more or less consistently since the mid-1970s. William Schambra, an important conservative thinker and participant in Reinventing Citizenship, the American Civic Forum, and the National Commission on Civic Renewal, noted in 1995, however, that previous Republican administrations had produced little more than a series of false starts. As Shambra argues, the Ford administration recognized the potency of the paradigm of "mediating structures," but its Office of Public Liaison's efforts to reach out to neighborhoods and civic associations degenerated into retail efforts to sell presidential initiatives. President Reagan waxed eloquent about returning initiative to local fraternal lodges and church groups but could manage little more than a Task Force on Private Sector Initiatives that engaged in debates on whether corporations should be expected to foot the bill for welfare state programs. President George H.W. Bush also proclaimed a grand vision of a nation of communities and voluntary organizations but produced only a modest "points of light" initiative aimed at conferring awards upon exemplary volunteer projects.

Along with Michael Joyce, whom he joined at the Bradley Foundation after leaving the Reagan administration, Schambra launched the "new citizenship" program to move beyond these false starts. Together they supported local projects and brought together conservative networks engaged in various efforts from the faith-based groups in urban ghettos to tenant management groups in public housing. Civic conservatives have emphasized moral reconstruction, as well as vouchers that they view as empowering parents by giving them choice in schools and social services. Some civic conservatives, however, have also come to recognize the important work of neighborhood associations, CDCs, and the IAF, as well as civic environmentalism. Stephen Goldsmith, who as Republican mayor of Indianapolis in the 1990s developed a variety of innovative civic partnerships, has brought a relatively broad perspective to these issues as an advisor to the current Bush administration.

This receptiveness of thinkers associated with both parties to broad themes of civic renewal, though still very selective, provides opportunities for movement building and policy development in the coming years. Opportunities, however, will not open up without further framing contests over what makes for robust civic engagement. How should government be involved and how much should be left to volunteerism? What is the balance between the civic production of public goods and individual market choice? Should we emphasize moral values or civic skills and organizational capacities? Is the new civics of collaboration about *compassion,* or is it fundamentally a question of *shared power?*

Answers to these and many other questions invariably spill over to the terrain of partisan politics, even as innovators and movement builders strive to guard the nonpartisan integrity of civic work in many settings. The civic renewal movement needs to manage these framing contests in a way that progressively refines its own frame, builds greater consensus on its core components, and melds them creatively with frames central to other movements, as well as to policy development and governance on a much broader scale. Movement thinkers and leaders also will need to mobilize their own partisan energies to further shape the dominant frames in the two major parties if more expansive opportunities for civic renewal are to open up in the coming years. In our view, Republican leaders will need to question whether compassionate conservatism, market choice, or moral fundamentalism can ever yield the civics for a complex democracy. And Democratic activists will have to question whether the new enthusiasm for the frame of liberal government as "nurturant parent" can ever inspire a self-governing people to produce and protect public goods on a broad scale.

In Conclusion

Much movement building occurs through everyday work and innovation in specific arenas. As civic entrepreneurs and activists refine their practice, frame it in the broad democratic terms they increasingly find in public and academic discourse, expand the range of stakeholders and coalition partners, and transfer their skills from one arena to another, they further build the foundations for a broad movement. In every specific arena, there is a wide range of potential capacity-building initiatives and policy designs that can help strengthen the civic renewal movement—initiatives, as well as obstacles, that are unfortunately beyond the scope of this book. Let us be absolutely clear that building capacity for faith-based community organizing, the civic mission of schools, and other arena-specific models must remain the foremost priority and that the integrity of movements such as the watershed movement, community youth development movement, and the movement to renew the civic mission of higher education must be nourished and protected in any attempt to build a more expansive civic renewal movement.

The danger, however, is that, without bolder movement-building and democratic reform projects, innovation will stall or remain segmented in specific arenas, fail to inspire broad enough engagement, and be unable to impel elites to alter their usual ways of doing business. Reviving the civic mission of K–12 schools and higher education, for instance, will fall far short of aspirations if we cannot provide avenues into other forms of robust civic problem solving after graduation. Successful faith-based community organizing, if segmented from other forms of community and youth development and environmental justice, will not fundamentally alter the contours of urban and regional planning and program design that disempower poor and moderate-income communities. Electoral and campaign finance reform and a sustained increase in voting, as important as these are, cannot address deeper problems of disengagement or modernize our civic infrastructure for the challenges of the twenty-first century.

Thus, even as movement building must remain acutely attuned to guarding the integrity of work and relationships in each specific arena, it must continue to explore bold proposals that attempt to leverage this work for larger democratic impact. The Saguaro Seminar, for instance, presents a package of proposals across the gamut of work, politics, religion, youth, and the arts to help orient a broad movement. We think it is essential to expand and deepen these proposals in a way that energizes actors in each arena, while keeping the broad, interconnected vista of renewal in view. Theda Skocpol offers what she calls "bold, even speculative recommendations" on media, elections, and tax incentives to help strengthen representative government responsive to "strong, encompassing associations." Bruce Ackerman and James Fishkin develop a bold proposal for a quadrennial national holiday that will help orient our presidential elections and policy debate around genuine democratic dialogue. Based on experience with deliberative polling, they have designed "deliberation day" as a national event preceding presidential elections and combining small group deliberations, larger assemblies, and a nationally televised debate. Our own proposal for a National Civic Congress, convening around the Fourth of July during major election cycles, would enable movement leaders, along with hundreds of teams of local innovators from every arena, to assemble in a festive celebration that showcases best practices in the national media and makes the stories of renewal a visible part of our civic culture—and thus help to motivate further civic initiative. The July Congress would strengthen networks across arenas, nurture a common movement identity, and enable scholars and practitioners to further explore policy designs to make government an effective catalyst for genuine self-government.

Other bold proposals and big designs will undoubtedly be offered. We ought to debate them vigorously, explore their limits, and build upon their strengths. Civic renewal is unlikely to happen simply through incremental steps in segmented arenas. We need to think big because our democratic life faces big problems. And because "democracy as a way of life" is a very big deal, indeed.

Part Four:

Research Note and Resource Guide

Research Note

Civic Renewal Organizations and Web Sites

Manuals, Best Practices, Declarations, and Proposals

Scholarly Studies

Research Note

T his book derives from our organizational research over a ten-year period, as well as the research and writing of many other scholars and practitioners. Here we present a selected set of scholarly resources, as well as manuals of best practices, civic declarations, commission reports, compendia of case studies and stories, and similar texts that have helped shape the development of the civic renewal movement. We also provide a selected list of Web sites for organizations engaged in civic innovation and movement building within specific arenas, as well as those concerned directly with the larger questions of democracy and civic renewal. Many documents are available on-line at the sponsoring organization's Web site or through links from the Civic Practices Network (www.cpn.org). While these resources represent only a slice of the knowledge and practice base, many more resources can be accessed through them. Scholarly sources are limited here primarily to published books.

Since this book addresses a wide readership of civic leaders, innovators, officials, and activists looking for the broader democratic meaning of their everyday public work, we dispense with the usual cumbersome forms of scholarly citation and debate. We hope that our annotations give requisite credit to those whose work has contributed so much to our own understanding, as well as to the field in general. We apologize to those whose work (especially scholarly articles) we draw upon but who are not adequately credited as much here as in our other writings. Within each arena, needless to say, there is a much more specialized literature and many hotly debated questions of effective practice, organizational strategy, policy design, and field building that a book such as this cannot tackle directly.

Our research teams at Brandeis University and the University of Wisconsin-Madison have been engaged in organizational research, interviews, fieldwork, and action research since 1993. Some of this research is presented in much greater detail in our books, *Civic Innovation in America* (2001) and *Public Journalism: Past and Future* (2003) and in various scholarly articles and research reports. Since these earlier books, we have conducted more than 200 new interviews and updated organizational data, as well as explored several new fields. For our research on youth civic engagement, we are especially grateful for the support of the Pew Charitable Trusts and the Center for Information and Research on Civic Learning and Engagement (CIRCLE).

To date, we have interviewed more than 700 civic innovators and movement builders. They are founders, leaders, and staff members of local, state, and national organizations and innovative programs within the fields we profile in this book. They are also community organizers, neighborhood association leaders, nonprofit directors and staff members, and youth activists. They are civic journalists, trainers, consultants, and foundation program officers. And they are federal, state, and local officials responsible for citizen participation programs.

We have convened or coconvened seven national strategy conferences of leading practitioners to reflect on best practices and movement building and have attended more than 150 other practitioner conferences, trainings, strategic planning retreats, national commission meetings, and board meetings of various networks. We have reviewed more than 350 community action guides, training curricula, and public agency handbooks and field guides. We have also examined directories of specific organizations and organizational fields and have reviewed organizational data provided in annual reports and project evaluations. In addition, we have reviewed the applications of more than 200 cities applying to the National Civic League for the All-America City Awards, which ask for detailed descriptions of three innovative civic projects, a self-evaluation according to NCL's *Civic Index,* and a general statement about approaches to community problem solving. We have also participated in the deliberations of national civic leaders to select finalists for these awards. For our civic journalism and youth civic engagement projects, we have conducted field research in 12 cities.

We have served in various other roles that combine scholarly research, strategic analysis, and movement building: senior advisor to the National Commission on Civic Renewal; advisory board member of CIRCLE; research director of Reinventing Citizenship and American Civic Forum; founding editors of the Civic Practices Network; "thought leader" for City Year; advisory board member for evaluation of Youth Leadership for Development Initiative; advisory board member of two year-long PBS Democracy Project series, *Citizens '96* and *Citizens State of the Union,* as well as the CBS Radio *Osgood File's* "Democracy, Citizenship, and Community" series, KERA's (PBS-Dallas) *Putting Communities First,* and the *Dallas Morning News* series on "The People's Movement." As consultants and advisors, we have benefited from working and sharing ideas with the following national associations and federal agencies in developing organizational strategies and projects: the National Civic League, Study Circles Resources Center, American Health Decisions, YMCA of the USA, American Planning Association, AARP, University Extension's National Public Policy Education Conference, as well as the U.S. Environmental Protection Agency, U.S. Department of Health and Human Services, Corporation for National and Community Service, and U.S. Department of

Housing and Urban Development. As engaged scholars, we have attempted to balance research with active involvement in these and other settings, though we have undoubtedly erred on one or another side on various occasions. We trust that our analysis here provides a fruitful enough mix to be useful to a broad range of citizens and hope that it will help expand our collective imagination of democratic possibilities.

We have accumulated many research debts over a decade of research, and we have acknowledged many of them in other writings. For the most recent research leading to this book and our work on youth civic engagement, we are especially grateful to research team coordinator Melissa Bass and to team members Jennifer Girotti, Anastasia Norton, Alexandra Piñeiros Shields, Elena Bayrock, Kirsten Moe, Kaitlin Nichols, Anna Jaffe-Desnick, Shauna Morimoto, Sheila Webb, and Benjamin Wutt. Peter Levine has offered critical insight on different parts of this research. William Galston has challenged us in important ways on our understanding of a broad civic renewal movement, even while providing many opportunities to contribute to it. Harry Boyte, as ever, has offered keen insight into the theory and practice of civic populism in many arenas. Elizabeth Hollander has been a great source of wisdom on the movement to renew the civic mission of higher education and its vital links to the broad civic renewal movement, as have John Saltmarsh and Barry Checkoway. Chris Gates and Derek Okubo of the National Civic League shared many insights about the movement, including hard-headed analyses of current obstacles. Susan Curnan, Alan Melchior, Andy Hahn, Della Hughes, and Cathy Burack of the Center for Youth and Communities at Brandeis University's Heller Graduate School for Social Policy and Management have housed much of our research on youth civic engagement and have nurtured us with their wisdom and extensive networks. Special thanks to Mary Heath of CYC for her financial management. David

Cunningham in the sociology department at Brandeis helped in our understanding of social movement theory. Peter Lee has been especially helpful in making sense of recent developments in the healthy communities movement. Matt Leighninger provided detailed comments on our manuscript and many questions for further thought. Henry Topper has provided critical insight on civic environmentalism and opened many doors for us at EPA. Mary Rouse and Randy Wallar of the Morgridge Center at the University of Wisconsin-Madison helped in our understanding of the service-learning field. The Johnson Foundation hosted our cosponsored conference on the information commons at the Wingspread center in Racine, Wisconsin, and many other conferences that have been important to the development of the broad civic renewal movement, as the various "Wingspread Declarations" clearly reveal. We are especially grateful to Christopher Beem of the Johnson Foundation. Steve Elkin of the Democracy Collaborative at the University of Maryland collaborated with us on this conference and also hosted a symposium in *PEGS: The Good Society* on our work on civic innovation. Jean Cohen, Bill Gamson, Mark R. Warren, Harry Boyte, and Susan Ostrander, who contributed to this symposium, have helped us sharpen our thinking in important ways.

Tobi Walker and Michael Delli Carpini, while at the Pew Charitable Trusts, provided critical support for us to convene four three-day movement-building strategy conferences among leading practitioners in the field of youth civic engagement, as well as for extensive interviews and organizational analysis. Robert Sherman of the Surdna Foundation provided much guidance on the field of youth civic engagement, of which his knowledge is encyclopedic, and his early support for the Civic Practices Network helped us begin to map innovations in various other fields as well. Cynthia Gibson of the Carnegie Corporation of New York has provided valuable feedback on our overall framing of the civic renewal movement. And the Kettering Foundation has offered research support and a most hospitable and stimulating environment in which to exchange ideas on civic innovation and democratic renewal. Special thanks go to David Mathews and John Dedrick, as well as to the board, for their critical insight.

We are most grateful to Andrea Walsh and Ellen Dawson-Witt for their critical feedback and careful editing.

Civic Renewal Organizations and Web Sites

Multipurpose Civic Renewal Organizations

National Civic League
www.ncl.org

Kettering Foundation
www.kettering.org

Center for Democracy and Citizenship
www.publicwork.org

Civic Practices Network
www.cpn.org

Democracy Collaborative
www.democracycollaborative.org

International Association for Public Participation
www.iap2.org

Innovations in Civic Participation
www.icicp.org

The Harwood Institute
www.theharwoodinstitute.org

Public Agenda
www.publicagenda.org

Pew Partnership for Civic Change
www.pew-partnership.org

Saguaro Seminar: Civic Engagement in America
www.ksg.harvard.edu/saguaro/

National Coalition for Dialogue and Deliberation
www.thataway.org

Community Organizing and Development

Industrial Areas Foundation
www.industrialareasfoundation.org

Study Circles Resource Center
www.studycircles.org

Assets-Based Community Development Institute
www.northwestern.edu/ipr/abcd.html

National Community Building Network
www.ncbn.org

Neighborhoods USA
www.nusa.org

Department of Neighborhoods, City of Seattle
www.cityofseattle.net/neighborhoods

(continued on the following page)

Community Organizing and Development, cont.

Office of Neighborhood Involvement, City of Portland
www.portlandonline.com/oni

National Youth Court Center
www.youthcourt.net

Center for Community Change
www.communitychange.org

Center for Neighborhood Technology
www.cnt.org

PICO
www.piconetwork.org

Gamaliel Foundation
www.gamaliel.org

Development Training Institute
www.dtinational.org

Project for Public Spaces
www.pps.org

Local Initiatives Support Corporation
www.liscnet.org

Enterprise Foundation
www.enterprisefoundation.org

National Congress for Community and Economic Development
www.ncced.org

Dudley Street Neighborhood Initiative
www.dsni.org

National Association for Community Mediation
www.nafcm.org

Association for Conflict Resolution
www.acresolution.org

National Center for Neighborhood Enterprise
www.ncne.com

National Conference for Community and Justice
www.nccj.org

Partnership for Livable Communities
www.livable.com

Families and Democracy Project
http://fsos.che.umn.edu/doherty/default.html

Putting Family First
www.puttingfamilyfirst.org

Center for Court Innovation
www.courtinnovation.org

Social Capital, Inc.
www.socialcapitalinc.org

Civic Environmentalism

River Network
www.rivernetwork.org

Earth Force
www.earthforce.org

Save The Bay
www.savebay.org

Restore America's Estuaries
www.estuaries.org

Alliance for Chesapeake Bay
www.acb-online.org

Chesapeake Bay Foundation
www.cbf.org

Land Trust Alliance
www.lta.org

Alternatives for Community and Environment
www.ace-ej.org

Campus Ecology
www.nwf.org/campusecology

North American Association for Environmental Education
www.naaee.org

Global Rivers Environmental Education Network
www.green.org

Project Learning Tree
www.plt.org

YMCA Earth Service Corps
www.yesc.org

Volunteer Stewardship Network
http://nature.org/wherewe-work/northamerica/states/illinois/volunteer

Chicago Wilderness
www.chicagowilderness.org

Student Conservation Association, Inc.
www.sca-inc.org

National Association of Service and Conservation Corps
www.nascc.org

The Nature Conservancy
http://nature.org

National Audubon Society
www.audubon.org

Center for the Rocky Mountain West
www.crmw.org

Forest Community Research
www.fcresearch.org

Lead Partnership Group
www.fcresearch.org/HTML/Projects/LeadPartner.html

Pacific West Community Forestry Center
www.fcresearch.org

National Network of Forest Practitioners
www.nnfp.org

(continued on the following page)

Civic Environmentalism, cont.

National Directory of Volunteer Monitoring Programs
http://yosemite.epa.gov/water/volmon.nsf/Home?readform

Urban Ecology Institute, Boston College
www.bc.edu/bc_org/research/urbaneco

The Food Project
www.thefoodproject.org

Massachusetts Watershed Coalition
www.commonwaters.org

Mattole Restoration Council
www.mattole.org

Engaged Campus

Campus Compact
www.compact.org

Office of University Partnerships/HUD
www.oup.org

Diversity Web
www.diversityweb.org

American Democracy Project
www.mtsu.edu/~amerdem
www.aascu.org/programs/adp

National Society for Experiential Education
www.nsee.org

American Association of State Colleges and Universities
www.aascu.org

Raise Your Voice
www.actionforchange.org

American Association for Higher Education
www.aahe.org

Campus Ecology
www.nwf.org/campusecology

Idealist on Campus
www.idealist.org

Community College National Center for Community Engagement
www.mc.maricopa.edu/other/engagement

Center for Liberal Education and Civic Engagement
www.compact.org/civic/CLECE/

Center for Community Partnerships, University of Pennsylvania
www.upenn.edu/ccp

Council on Public Engagement, University of Minnesota
www.umn.edu/civic

(continued on the following page)

Engaged Campus, cont.

National Service-Learning
Clearinghouse
www.servicelearning.org

Association of American Colleges
and Universities
www.aacu.org

Center for Academic Excellence,
Portland State University
www.oaa.pdx.edu/cae/cup.htm

Michigan Journal of Community
Service Learning
www.umich.edu/~mjcsl

New England Resource
Center for
Higher Education
www.nerche.org

Project Pericles

www.projectpericles.org

Learn and Serve, Corporation for
National and Community Service
www.learnandserve.org

Public Issues Education,
Cooperative Extension
www.publicissueseducation.net

Youth Vote Coalition
www.youthvote.org

American Political
Science Association, Civic
Education Network
www.apsanet.org/CENnet

American Sociological
Association, Task Force
on Public Sociologies
coserver.uhw.utoledo.edu/pubsoc

Community Youth Development and Civic Education

Center for Information and
Research on Civic Learning and
Engagement (CIRCLE)
www.civicyouth.org

Innovation Center for Community
and Youth Development
www.theinnovationcenter.org

Alternatives, Inc.
www.altinc.org

Public Achievement
www.publicachievement.org

Forum for Youth Investment
www.forumforyouthinvestment.org

National Center for Learning and
Citizenship, Education
Commission of the States
www.ecs.org/nclc

YMCA of the USA
www.ymcacivicengagement.org

AmeriCorps
www.americorps.org

(continued on the following page)

189

Community Youth Development and Civic Education, cont.

Campaign for the Civic Mission of Schools
www.civicmissionofschools.org

Center for Civic Education
www.civiced.org

Center for Youth as Resources
www.cyar.org

Center for Youth Development, Academy for Educational Development
www.aed.org/Youth

Close Up Foundation
www.closeup.org

Institute for Cultural Affairs
www.igc.org/ica

Constitutional Rights Foundation
www.crf-usa.org

CYD Journal
www.cydjournal.org

Do Something
www.DoSomething.org

Hampton Coalition for Youth
www.hampton.gov

Boston-area Youth Organizing Project
www.byop.org

National Youth Advocacy Coalition
www.nyacyouth.org

Learn and Serve America
www.learnandserve.org

Learning In Deed
www.learningindeed.org

National Alliance for Civic Education
www.cived.net

Funders Collaborative on Youth Organizing
www.fcyo.org

National Conference for Community and Justice
www.nccj.org

National 4-H Council
www.fourhcouncil.org

National Network for Youth
www.nn4youth.org

National Service-Learning Clearinghouse
www.servicelearning.org

National Service-Learning Partnership
www.service-learningpartnership.org

National Youth Court Center
www.youthcourt.net

National Youth Leadership Council
www.nylc.org

Search Institute
www.search-institute.org

(continued on the following page)

Community Youth Development and Civic Education, cont.

Rock the Vote
www.rockthevote.org

Project 540
www.project540.org

Corporation for National and Community Service
www.nationalservice.org

Street Law
www.streetlaw.org

YouthBuild USA
www.youthbuild.org

San Francisco Youth Commission
www.sfgov.org/site/youth_commission_index.asp

Youth Leadership Institute
www.yli.org

Youth on Board
www.youthonboard.org

Philanthropy for Active Civic Engagement
www.gfcns.org

Coalition of Community Foundations for Youth
www.ccfy.org

Public Allies
www.publicallies.org

City Year
www.cityyear.org

National Association of Service and Conservation Corps
www.nascc.org

American Association of State Service Commissions
www.asc-online.org

LISTEN, Inc.
www.lisn.org

Healthy Communities and Health Decisions

**Association for Community
Health Improvement**
www.communityhlth.org

**Massachusetts Regional Centers
for Healthy Communities**
www.state.ma.us/dph/ohc/
reghealthcenters.htm

**California Healthy Cities and
Communities**
www.civicpartnerships.org

**Community-Campus Partnerships
for Health**
http://depts.washington.edu/ccph

CityNet Healthy Cities
www.iupui.edu/~citynet/cnet.html

**International Healthy
Cities Foundation**
www.healthycities.org

Solano Coalition for Better Health
www.solanocoalition.org

Interfaith Health Program
www.ihpnet.org

American Health Decisions
www.ahd.org

Oregon Health Decisions
http://oregonhealthdecisions.org

California Health Decisions
www.cahd.org

Deliberative Democracy and Dialogue

National Issues Forums Institute
www.nifi.org

Study Circles Resource Center
www.studycircles.org

America*Speaks*
www.americaspeaks.org

**Dialogue to Action Initiative,
National Coalition for Dialogue
and Deliberation**
www.thataway.org

Co-Intelligence Institute
www.co-intelligence.org

Public Conversations Project
www.publicconversations.org

Center for Deliberative Polling
www.la.utexas.edu/research/delpol

Public Journalism and Civic Communications

Institute for Interactive Journalism
www.j-lab.org

Center for Digital Democracy
www.democraticmedia.org

Civic Practices Network
http://www.cpn.org/topics/communication

Free Expression Policy Project
www.fepproject.org

American Library Association
www.ala.org

Gotham Gazette
www.gothamgazette.com

Pew Center for Civic Journalism
(on-line archive)
www.pewcenter.org

PressThink: Ghost of Democracy in the Media Machine
http://journalism.nyu.edu/pubzone/weblogs/pressthink

Public Knowledge
www.publicknowledge.org

PJNet
http://www.pjnet.org

e-the People
www.e-thepeople.org

Community Technology Centers Network
www.ctcnet.org

Youth Noise
www.youthNOISE.com

Harlem Live
http://www.harlemlive.org

Street-Level Youth Media
http://streetlevel.iit.edu

Free Culture
http://www.freeculture.org/

Free Press
http://www.freepress.net/

Alliance for Community Media
http://www.alliancecm.org/

Center for Media Literacy
http://www.medialit.org

Creative Commons
http://creativecommons.org/

Center for Social Media
http://www.centerforsocialmedia.org/

Consumers Union
http://www.consumersunion.org/phonesandmedia.html

Hear Us Now
http://www.hearusnow.org/

Manuals, Best Practices, Declarations, and Proposals

Civic Renewal: General

Ackerman, Bruce and James Fishkin. 2004. *Deliberation Day.* New Haven, CT: Yale University Press.

    As a result of their experience with deliberative polling, two prominent political scientists have designed "deliberation day" as a national event preceding presidential elections and combining small group deliberations, larger assemblies, and a nationally televised debate.

Boyte, Harry, Benjamin Barber, Will Marshall, and Carmen Sirianni. 1994. *Civic Declaration: A Call for a New Citizenship.* Dayton, OH: Kettering Foundation.

    Drawing on several national collaborative projects among leading civic innovators, as well as key partners in government, this declaration provides an initial statement of the themes of the civic renewal movement. *On-line.*

Gardner, John. 1995. *National Renewal.* Washington, DC and Denver, CO: Independent Sector and National Civic League.

    Founder of Common Cause and Independent Sector and former chair of the National Civic League, the late John Gardner elaborates core principles of the civic renewal movement in its early stages. *On-line.*

Greenberg, Stanley and Theda Skocpol (eds.). 1997. *The New Majority: Toward a Popular Progressive Politics.* New Haven, CT: Yale University Press.

Among a range of political and policy proposals are several (especially those of Weir and Ganz, and Skocpol) that include a civic reframing intended to guide progressives.

Kesler, John T. and Drew O'Connor. 2001. "The American Communities Movement," *National Civic Review* 90:4 (Winter), 295–305.

Based on daylong dialogues among leaders in various community-based movements, these two nationally prominent practitioners found, despite limited cross-movement collaboration, much commonality in themes, enormous potential to learn from each other, virtually unanimous enthusiasm for an integrative movement, though not much interest in merging agendas and identities. The glaring absence of a convening forum was noted.

Lappé, Frances Moore and Paul Martin DuBois. 1994. *The Quickening of America: Rebuilding Our Nation, Remaking Our Lives.* San Francisco, CA: Jossey-Bass.

This highly usable guide can help citizens reimagine their roles as practical public problem solvers. It covers a broad range of techniques, as well as essential concepts such as power, self-interest, and public dialogue.

Leighninger, Matthew. 2005. *The Next Form of Democracy: How Local Civic Experiments Are Shaping the Future of Politics.* Memphis, TN: Vanderbilt University Press.

Following rich experience with study circles in various cities, the author offers a model of democratic organizing that includes public officials as partners with citizens in deliberative problem solving.

Loeb, Paul. 2001. *Soul of a Citizen: Living with Conviction in a Cynical Time.* New York, NY: St. Martin's Press.

Loeb offers a book of inspiring stories of citizen action and personal commitment from many arenas of social life.

Marshall, Will, Al From, William Galston, and Doug Ross. 1997. "The New Progressive Declaration: A Political Philosophy for the Information Age," 17–35 in *Building the Bridge: Ten Big Ideas to Transform America,* Will Marshall (ed.). Lanham, MD: Rowman and Littlefield.

This declaration from the Progressive Policy Institute offers a governing philosophy rooted deeply in civic empowerment and a broad movement for democratic renewal.

National Commission on Civic Renewal. 1998. *A Nation of Spectators: How Civic Disengagement Weakens America and What We Can Do About It.* Final Report of the National Commission on Civic Renewal. College Park, MD: University of Maryland.

Directed by William Galston, the national commission brought together prominent liberals and conservatives to develop some areas of consensus on the challenges of civic renewal and garnered further public recognition for the emergent civic renewal movement. *On-line.*

Saguaro Seminar. 2000. *Better Together: Civic Engagement in America.* Cambridge, MA: Kennedy School of Government, Harvard University.

Cochaired by Robert Putnam, author of *Bowling Alone;* Lewis Feldstein; and Christopher Gates, president of the National Civic League; these civic, political, and academic leaders argue that "we need nothing less than a sustained, broad-based social movement" to rebuild our civic infrastructure. The report offers a set of very sensible proposals to enable ordinary Americans from all walks of life to contribute through small but meaningful steps. "Every institution must make building social capital a principal goal and core value." *On-line.*

Schambra, William. 1994. "By The People: The Old Values of the New Citizenship," *Policy Review* (Summer), 32–38.

This is a formative statement by a leading conservative thinker in the debate about the new citizenship and civic renewal.

Sirianni, Carmen and Lewis Friedland. 2002. "The National Civic Congress: A Proposal for Movement Building," *National Civic Review* 91:1 (Spring), 81–94.

This proposal for a National Civic Congress, to be convened regularly around the Fourth of July and to include hundreds of teams of innovators from every arena and part of the country, is designed to showcase best practices, build networks, explore policy design, and shape media discourse on civic problem solving. The July Congress aims at building the civic renewal movement within the constraints discussed in Part Three of this book.

Community Organizing and Development

Atlee, Tom. 2003. *The Tao of Democracy: Using Co-Intelligence to Create a World That Works for All.* Cranston, RI: The Writer's Collective.

As a lifelong peace and social justice activist who, not atypically, has moved from protest politics to collaborative action, the author explores a variety of methods by which citizens can develop a culture of dialogue to grapple with social complexity.

Briand, Michael K. 1999. *Practical Politics: Five Principles for a Community That Works.* Urbana and Chicago, IL: University of Illinois Press.

Drawing on a broad range of research and innovation, this book develops five core principles (inclusion, comprehension, deliberation, realism, and public judgment/action) for revitalizing democracy in communities.

Chambers, Edward T., Michael A. Cowan, and Studs Terkel. 2003. *Roots for Radicals: Organizing for Power, Action, and Justice.* New York, NY: Continuum International.

The executive director of the Industrial Areas Foundation and his collaborators examine core principles of faith-based community organizing.

Cortes, Ernesto, Jr. 1993. "Reweaving the Fabric: The Iron Rule and the IAF Strategy for Power and Politics," 294–319 in *Interwoven Destinies: Cities and the Nation.* Henry Cisneros (ed.). New York, NY: Norton.

One of the preeminent faith-based community organizers examines core concepts of power, self-interest, and public relationship in the Industrial Areas Foundation (IAF) network. *On-line.*

Diers, Jim. 2004. *Neighborhood Power: Building Community the Seattle Way.* Seattle, WA: University of Washington Press.

The founding director of the Seattle Department of Neighborhoods provides rich profiles of citizen empowerment through community planning, neighborhood matching funds, community gardening, and other programs.

Doherty, William J. 2002. "The Citizen Therapist and the Civic Renewal Movement." Minneapolis: University of Minnesota.

The founder of the Families and Democracy Project examines the ways in which family therapists can expand their imagination of how to do civic work with families and communities. This piece represents civic professionalism at its best—and with a broad movement perspective. It was originally presented to the National Council of Schools and Programs in Professional Psychology. *On-line.*

Doherty, William J. and Jason S. Carroll. 2002. "The Families and Democracy Project." *Family Process* 41:4, 579–90.

In response to a critique of the traditional provider/consumer models of family services, the authors offer case studies of families and communities reclaiming control over their daily lives. The studies address issues such as the overscheduling of kids (Putting Family First) and caring for ill family members (Partners in Diabetes). Professionals work in collaboration, using the public work model of the Center for Democracy and Citizenship and lessons from faith-based community organizing. *On-line.*

Gastil, John and Peter Levine. 2005. *The Deliberative Democracy Handbook: Strategies for Effective Civic Engagement in the Twenty-First Century.* San Francisco, CA: Jossey-Bass.

This essential collection by practitioners and scholars provides a broad overview of the field, as well as a focused discussion of distinct models.

Gecan, Michael. 2002. *Going Public.* Boston, MA: Beacon.

Written by a prominent IAF organizer, this book serves as an in-depth guide to the philosophy and practice of faith-based community organizing and is especially rich in its stories of everyday politics.

Goldsmith, Stephen. 2002. *Putting Faith in Neighborhoods: Making Cities Work through Grassroots Citizenship.* Noblesville, IN: Hudson Institute.

An advisor to President George W. Bush on community-based strategies tells the story of "municipal citizenship" and urban revitalization during the author's tenure as mayor of Indianapolis in the

1990s. He focuses especially on partnerships with neighborhood organizations and faith-based groups.

Grogan, Paul and Tony Proscio. 2000. *Comeback Cities: A Blueprint for Urban Revival.* Boulder, CO: Westview Press.

The former director of the Local Initiatives Support Corporation teams up with a journalist to harvest key lessons of urban renewal based on community development strategies in housing, credit, local business, and community policing.

Henton, Douglas, John Melville, and Kimberly Walesh. 1997. *Grassroots Leaders for a New Economy: How Civic Entrepreneurs Are Building Prosperous Communities.* San Francisco, CA: Jossey-Bass.

Three advisors to Joint Venture: Silicon Valley, an innovative partnership of business, government, education, and community leaders, examine how civic entrepreneurship and a shared vision in various cities, regions, and states can foster local economic development and renewal. The authors view market actors as embedded civic actors.

Kemmis, Daniel. 1995. *The Good City and the Good Life: Renewing the Sense of Community.* Boston, MA: Houghton Mifflin.

The former Democratic mayor of Missoula, Montana, an influential voice in the civic renewal movement, examines the role of the "good citizen" and the "good politician" in the life of his city and others like it.

Kingsley, G. Thomas, Joseph McNeely, and James Gibson. 1996. *Community Building: Coming of Age.* Baltimore, MD and Washington, DC: The Development Training Institute and the Urban Institute.

This report examines the core themes of the community-building movement and offers important recommendations for strengthening it through a national campaign, federal and local supports, and local intermediary organizations. *On-line.*

Kretzmann, John P. and John L. McKnight. 1997. *Building Communities from the Inside Out.* Chicago, IL:ACTA Publications.

This wonderful guide, which has sold more than 100,000 copies since it first appeared in 1993, presents hundreds of examples and mapping exercises for locating and mobilizing community assets. This basic text of the assets-based community development approach has a companion video training program called Mobilizing Community Assets.

Lipman, Mark and Leah Mahan. 1996. *Holding Ground: The Rebirth of Dudley Street.* Boston, MA: Holding Ground Productions (Distributed by New Day Films).

This one-hour documentary, which aired on PBS, tells the lively story of the Dudley Street Neighborhood Initiative's efforts to organize the community and rebuild a part of inner-city Boston.

Lukensmeyer, Carolyn J. and Steve Brigham. 2002. "Taking Democracy to Scale: Creating a Town Hall Meeting for the Twenty-First Century." *National Civic Review* 91:4 (Winter), 351–66.

Two leaders of America*Speaks* outline the essential components (small group dialogue, networked computers, theming, electronic keypads, large video screens) of this model and show their application in Listening to the City, a dialogue in which more than 4,000 citizens contributed important design elements for rebuilding Ground Zero.

Mathews, David and Noëlle McAfee. 2002. *Making Choices Together: The Power of Public Deliberation.* Dayton, OH: Kettering Foundation.

Based on extensive experience with National Issues Forums and other forms of public dialogue, this guide provides a wonderful introduction to the concept and practice of deliberative democracy.

Mathews, David. 2002. *For Communities to Work.* Dayton, OH: Kettering Foundation.

This monograph examines how an engaged public is vital to problem solving in communities, especially when confronted with "wicked problems."

National Civic League. 2000. *Community Visioning and Strategic Planning Handbook.* Denver, CO: National Civic League.

This indispensable handbook provides a step-by-step guide to creating a sustainable vision and action plan for communities. From the logistical planning of the initiating committee to the implementation of the community plan, communities learn how to engage broad-based community participation, evaluate their civic infrastructure, and effect outcomes for their desired future. *On-line.*

National Civic League. 1999. *The Civic Index: Measuring Your Community's Civic Health.* Denver, CO: National Civic League.

  This revised edition of *The Civic Index* is a widely used twelve-point community self-evaluation tool. *The Civic Index* assesses civic infrastructure, those characteristics that communities possess to solve problems effectively. *On-line.*

Neumark, Heidi. 2003. *Breathing Space: A Spiritual Journey in the South Bronx.* Boston, MA: Beacon.

  The former pastor of Transfiguration Lutheran Church (a predominantly Hispanic and African American congregation) tells the story of how faith-based community organizing enabled these inner-city residents to rebuild their neighborhoods, strengthen their faith, and restore their hope for a just and democratic future.

Pew Partnership for Civic Change. 1998. "Just Call It Effective" *Civic Change—Moving from Projects to Progress.* Charlottesville, VA: University of Richmond.

  Supported by the Pew Partnership in the mid-1990s, this report presents an extensive series of lessons of civic change in 14 smaller cities. *On-line.*

Project for Public Spaces. 2000. *How to Turn a Place Around.* New York, NY: Project for Public Spaces.

  Based on 30 years of experience in urban design, architecture, and landscaping, this guide enables professionals and citizens to collaborate in designing public spaces for inclusive community interaction and participation. A companion video, *How to Create Great Streets and Public Spaces,* is also available.

Rahtz, Howard. 2001. *Community Policing: A Handbook for Beat Cops and Supervisors.* Monsey, NY: Criminal Justice Press.

  This handbook, which draws on examples of community policing, is designed for the training academy as well as everyday beat work and supervision.

Ott, Gerald. *The New Challenges of American Immigration: What Should We Do?* Dayton, OH: Kettering Foundation.

  One among many of the National Issues Forums' issue books and moderator guides for public discussion of national issues with local relevance, this serves as a companion to the public television series *The New Americans. On-line.*

Study Circles Resource Center. 2001. *Organizing Community-wide Dialogue for Action and Change: A Step-By-Step Guide.* Pomfret, CT: Study Circles Resource Center.

This detailed guide, which represents a wealth of wisdom in study circle practice, is designed to be used, if need be, with minimal facilitation by SCRC. *On-line.*

_____. 1997. *Facing the Challenge of Race and Race Relations: Democratic Dialogue and Action for Stronger Communities.* Third edition. Pomfret, CT: Study Circles Resource Center.

Drawing on extensive work on racism in many settings, this guide seeks to enable communities with tough racial divisions to come together to bridge boundaries and develop productive strategies. *On-line.*

_____. 1998. *A Guide for Training Study Circle Facilitators.* Pomfret, CT: Study Circles Resource Center.

This highly user-friendly guide provides a step-by-step method for training and recruiting facilitators (including youth) for communitywide study circles projects. *On-line.*

Susskind, Lawrence, Sarah McKearnan, and Jennifer Thomas-Larmer (eds.). 1999. *The Consensus Building Handbook: A Comprehensive Guide to Reaching Agreement.* Thousand Oaks, CA: Sage.

Informed by a wealth of reflective practice, this collection provides general overviews and case studies of a broad array of models in the consensus-building field.

Yankelovich, Daniel. 1999. *The Magic of Dialogue: Transforming Conflict into Cooperation.* New York, NY: Simon and Schuster.

Drawing on years of experience with public opinion research, as well as with deliberative dialogue through Public Agenda, the author offers principles and practices relevant not only to communities, but also to businesses and other organizations in an increasingly complex and diverse world.

Civic Environmentalism

Barlett, Peggy and Geoffrey Chase (eds.). 2004. *Sustainability on Campus: Stories and Strategies for Change.* Cambridge, MA: MIT Press.

Based on innovations at various colleges and universities, this collection features essays by faculty, administrators, staff, and students in the forefront of the growing movement for environmental responsibility on campuses. It reveals the "messy reality of participatory engagement in cultural transformation."

Bolling, David. M. 1994. *How to Save a River: A Handbook for Citizen Action.* Washington, DC: Island Press.

This guide offers basic tools for developing watershed organizations, finding allies, building public support, and conducting campaigns.

Earth Force. 1999. *Earth Force Community Action and Problem Solving: Teacher Manual.* Alexandria, VA: Earth Force.

This detailed curriculum guide, which draws on a wealth of good practice in service learning, environmental education, and civic education, is attentive to forming genuine partnerships between schools and community groups.

_____. 2001. *Protecting Our Watersheds: Teachers' Guide.* Alexandria, VA: Earth Force.

This is a widely used guide designed to support student work on watersheds through Global Rivers Environmental Education Network.

_____. 1999. *Earth Force CAPS: Community Action and Problem Solving.* Alexandria, VA: Earth Force.

This is an excellent manual to help guide youth community problem solving on the environment.

Federal Interagency Working Group on Environmental Justice. 2002. *Environmental Justice Collaborative Model: A Framework to Ensure Local Problem Solving.* Washington, DC: U.S. Environmental Protection Agency.

Composed of representatives of 11 federal agencies, this working group explores the collaborative model that has recently gained much ground in the EJ movement and in agency practice. It includes case studies from a broad range of agencies and community partners.

Firehock, Karen, Fran Flanigan, and Pat Devlin. 2002. *Community Watershed Forums: A Planner's Guide.* Baltimore, MD: Alliance for Chesapeake Bay.

    Based on years of experience with Chesapeake Bay watershed groups, this hands-on guide provides steps for convening citizens and multiple organizational stakeholders to develop a shared vision and collaborative restoration strategy. *On-line.*

House, Freeman. 1999. *Totem Salmon: Life Lessons from Another Species.* Boston, MA: Beacon.

    The founder of the Mattole Restoration Council in northern California, an important model for watershed restoration, tells an inspired story of its meticulous work and the lessons of community collaboration.

Kemmis, Daniel. 2001. *This Sovereign Land: A New Vision for Governing the West.* Washington, DC: Island Press.

    This provocative book by former Democratic speaker of the Montana House of Representatives, mayor of Missoula, and lifelong environmentalist, argues that national authority over public lands in the West must yield to regional sovereignty rooted in the new collaborative forms of ecosystem governance that have been growing so quickly in recent years and that represent a "collaboration movement" with profound democratic implications.

Landy, Marc, Megan M. Susman, and Debra S. Knopman. 1999. *Civic Environmentalism in Action: A Field Guide to Regional and Local Initiatives.* Washington, DC: Progressive Policy Institute.

    Leading analysts in the development of the paradigm present a variety of examples and approaches.

Lee, Charles. Forthcoming. "Collaborative Models to Achieve Environmental Justice and Healthy Communities." In David Pellow and Robert Brulle (eds.). *People, Power, and Pollution: A Critical Appraisal of the Environmental Justice Movement.* Cambridge, MA: MIT Press.

An early leader in the EJ movement and current chair of the Federal Interagency Working Group on Environmental Justice profiles a second generation of leaders operating within the new EJ collaborative paradigm, including Mary Nelson of Bethel New Life, Harold Mitchell of ReGenesis, and others.

Lerner, Steve. 1997. *Eco-Pioneers: Practical Visionaries Solving Today's Environmental Problems.* Cambridge, MA: MIT Press.

A journalist richly profiles innovators from a variety of settings, such as environmental justice, watersheds, and sustainable communities and campuses.

National Environmental Justice Advisory Council. 2003. *Advancing Environmental Justice through Pollution Prevention.* Washington, DC: U.S. Environmental Protection Agency.

This report, representing a significant change in EJ movement thinking, examines various pathways to environmental justice through pollution prevention and urges the adoption of multistakeholder collaborative models and increased participation and capacity building at the community and tribal levels. *On-line.*

_____. 2004. *Ensuring Risk Reduction in Communities with Multiple Stressors: Environmental Justice and Cumulative Risks/Impacts.* Washington, DC: U.S. Environmental Protection Agency.

This report, which represents a continued shift in the movement, recommends that the "environmental justice collaborative problem-solving model" should be widely institutionalized as the primary way to reduce multiple, aggregate, and cumulative risks faced by disadvantaged communities. *On-line.*

River Network. N.d. *Starting Up: A Handbook for New River and Watershed Organizations.* Portland, OR: River Network.

This large compendium of tools provides extensive guidance about establishing an effective watershed organization.

River Network and Rivers, Trails, and Conservation Assistance Program of the National Parks Service. 2003. *2003 River and Watershed Conservation Directory.* Portland, OR, and Washington, DC: River Network and RTCA.

The most comprehensive national directory of watershed associations and kindred citizen groups, public agencies, and centers. *On-line.*

Save America's Estuaries and Estuarine Research Foundation. 1999. *Principles of Estuarine Habitat Restoration: Working Together to Restore America's Estuaries.* Arlington, VA, and Port Republic, MD: RAE-ERF.

These principles combine sound science, adaptive management, multistakeholder partnerships, and citizen engagement in all aspects of the restoration process, including design, implementation, and monitoring. It includes short case studies. *On-line.*

Stapp, William B., Arjen E.J. Wals, and Sheri L. Stankorb. 1996. *Environmental Education for Empowerment: Action Research and Community Problem Solving.* Ann Arbor, MI: Global Rivers Environmental Education Network.

This guide by a pioneering environmental educator is oriented toward democratic problem solving in communities and the full participation of youth.

Stevens, William. 1995. *Miracle Under the Oaks: The Revival of Nature in America.* New York, NY: Pocket Books.

Written by a *New York Times* science writer, this beautiful account details the everyday practices and citizen science behind the Volunteer Stewardship Network's prairie and wildflower restoration work in the Chicago metropolitan area, a model for many in the restoration and land trust movements.

Wondolleck, Julia M. and Steven L. Yaffee. 2000. *Making Collaboration Work: Lessons from Innovation in Natural Resource Management.* Washington, DC: Island Press.

This book presents systematic, practical lessons on collaborative problem solving as an essential feature of ecosystem management and is based on extensive surveys of ongoing work in many different agencies and with various conservation groups over a ten-year period. It also addresses the concerns of critics of collaborative approaches.

YMCA Earth Service Corps, National Resource Center. 2000. *YMCA Earth Service Corps Administrator's Guide and Club Handbook.* Second edition. Chicago, IL: National Council of Young Men's Christian Associations of the USA.

 Based on a decade of experience, this important handbook provides local Y's with concrete tools for developing community-based service learning on the environment and partnerships with schools.

Engaged Campus

Battistoni, Richard M. 2002. *Civic Engagement Across the Curriculum: A Resource Book for Service-Learning Faculty in All Disciplines.* Providence, RI: Campus Compact.

 This guides offers core conceptual and practical tools for incorporating service learning and engaged citizenship into university curricula.

Boyte, Harry and Elizabeth Hollander. 1999. *Wingspread Declaration on the Civic Responsibilities of Research Universities.* Racine, WI: Johnson Foundation.

 This important declaration has shaped the development of the civic renewal movement in higher education. *On-line.*

Ehrlich, Thomas and Elizabeth Hollander. 1999. *Presidents' Fourth of July Declaration on the Civic Responsibility of Higher Education.* Providence, RI: Campus Compact.

 Endorsed by the Presidential Leadership Colloquium convened by Campus Compact and the American Council of Education, this declaration represents the most important short statement of vision and principles in the movement to renew the civic mission of higher education. *On-line.*

Gelmon, Sherril B., Barbara A. Holland, Amy Driscoll, Amy Spring, and Seanna Kerrigan. 2001. *Assessing Service Learning and Civic Engagement: Principles and Techniques.* Providence, RI: Campus Compact.

Written by prominent leaders in the field, this is an indispensable guide for assessing the impact of service learning and civic engagement on students, faculty, institutions, and communities.

Heffernan, Kerrissa. 2001. *Fundamentals of Service-Learning Course Construction.* Providence, RI: Campus Compact.

This manual provides general guidance as well as many specific models of service-learning syllabi from colleges and universities across the country.

Jacoby, Barbara and Associates. 2003. *Building Partnerships for Service Learning.* San Francisco, CA: Jossey-Bass.

Based on rich case studies from varied university and community settings, this important collection of essays examines how to create sustainable, reciprocal, and democratic partnerships.

Kellogg Commission on the Future of State and Land-Grant Universities. 1999. *Returning to Our Roots: The Engaged Institution.* Washington, DC: National Association of State Universities and Land-Grant Colleges.

Composed of some two dozen presidents, the Kellogg Commission has emphasized the engaged campus as a core element in renewing the covenant of land-grant universities. *On-line.*

Long, Sarah H. 2002. *The New Student Politics: The Wingspread Statement on Student Civic Engagement.* Providence, RI: Campus Compact.

Based on the national student summit convened by Campus Compact, this declaration analyzes why many students feel alienated from traditional politics yet also find many forms of community service inadequate. Building on their experiences in service learning and university-community partnerships, the students call for more robust forms of relational politics and coproduction ("service politics") to create new bridges to productive civic and political engagement. *On-line.*

National Forum on Higher Education for the Public Good. 2003. *Higher Education for the Public Good: A Report from the National Leadership Dialogues.* Ann Arbor, MI: Center for the Study of Higher Education and Postsecondary Education, University of Michigan.

This report by Scott London captures the rich discussion on the civic mission of higher education that emerged at three leadership dialogues and a national summit among more than 200 higher education leaders, joined by various public officials and community organizers. Discussions linked innovation in the university to the broader civic renewal movement and to the task of developing democratic leadership broadly in communities, institutions, and professions. It also developed a common action agenda. *On-line.*

National Public Policy Education Committee, Cooperative Extension. 2002. *Public Issues Education: Increasing Competence, Enabling Communities.* Cooperative Extension.

Proceeding on the assumption that traditional expert-based Extension education proves inadequate in solving problems that are complex, uncertain, and subject to public disagreement, this guide seeks to orient Cooperative Extension educators and administrators toward engaging the public in deliberative and collaborative problem solving. The guide includes a broad range of issues from land use, water quality, and food safety to health care and economic development. It explores the roles of Extension professionals as civic networkers, convenors, and facilitators, as well as researchers and program designers. *On-line.*

Nyden, Philip, Anne Figert, Mark Shibley, and Darryl Burrows (eds.). 1997. *Building Community: Social Science in Action.* Thousand Oaks, CA: Pine Forge Press.

This collection of essays examines the practice of university-community collaboration in research that makes a difference in urban communities on issues ranging from fair lending and neighborhood revitalization to toxic chemicals and AIDS prevention.

Peters, Scott and Margo Hittleman (eds.). 2003. *We Grow People: Profiles of Extension Educators.* Ithaca, NY: Cornell University Cooperative Extension.

These rich profiles explore how university Extension educators are reinventing the public dimensions of their work and identities and engaging with communities as civic professionals. *On-line.*

Pew Partnership for Civic Change (ed.). 2004. *New Directions in Civic Engagement: University Avenue Meets Main Street.* Richmond, VA: University of Richmond.

This collection of essays brings together some 20 leaders in higher education and community development to reflect on the challenges of community/university partnerships in a variety of institutional settings ranging from community colleges and schools of theology to Ivy League universities and historically black colleges.

Strand, Kerry, Sam Marullo, Nick Cutforth, Randy Stoecker, and Patrick Donohue. 2003. *Community-Based Research and Higher Education: Principles and Practices.* San Francisco: Jossey-Bass.

This excellent guide examines a broad range of practices in community-based research, the challenges of building fruitful and sustainable partnerships between academic researchers and community organizations, and the engagement of undergraduates in work that delivers substantial value, especially to marginalized communities.

Community Youth Development and K-12 Civic Education

Backer, Thomas E. and Cynthia Kunz. 2003. *Creating the Future: The Story of 4-H's National Conversation on Youth Development in the 21st Century.* Chevy Chase, MD: National 4-H Council.

This report details the planning and convening of the 2001–2002 county, state, and national conversations among adults and youth, which were designed to reposition the 4-H movement around youth civic engagement. The report also examines lessons from the process, including ongoing change in 4-H programs and governance. *On-line.*

Bass, Melissa. 1999. *Public Adventures: An Active Citizenship Curriculum for Youth.* Madison, WI: 4-H Cooperative Curriculum System.

Based on work within the 4-H system and other innovative programs, this curriculum is designed to help youth contribute to the world around them and develop a lifelong commitment to active citizenship. The heart of Public Adventures is the projects, planned by youth themselves, that create, change, or improve something of value to a broad public.

Carlson, Cindy and Elizabeth Sykes. 2001. *Shaping the Future: Working Together, Changing Communities. A Manual on How to Start or Improve Your Own Youth Commission.* Hampton, VA: Hampton Coalition for Youth.

    Based on lessons of one of the most successful citywide systems of youth civic engagement, this manual provides students with detailed hands-on knowledge of how to establish and run youth commissions and advisory boards.

Center for Civic Education. N.d. *We the People … Project Citizen.* Calabasas, CA: Center for Civic Education.

    This middle-school curriculum, administered in cooperation with the National Conference of State Legislatures, engages students in learning how to monitor and influence public policy at the local and state level through collaborative classroom work. Students present final portfolios to other classes, parents, and community groups and can enter them into local, state, and national competitions.

_____. N.d. *We the People … The Citizen and the Constitution.* Calabasas, CA: Center for Civic Education.

    Designed for elementary, middle school, and high school, this curriculum focuses on the history of the U.S. Constitution and Bill of Rights and includes problem-solving and cooperative-learning techniques to help develop the participatory skills of citizens.

Constitutional Rights Foundation and Close Up Foundation. 1995. *Active Citizenship Today (ACT).* Los Angeles, CA: Constitutional Rights Foundation.

    The ACT service-learning curriculum and guides for grades 5–12 are designed to enable students to define their community's problems, assess resources, examine policy options, and take action.

Dingerson, Leigh and Sarah H. Hay. 1998. *Co/Motion: Guide to Youth-Led Social Change.* Washington, DC: Alliance for Justice.

    This guide on youth organizing draws from the Alinsky tradition of community organizing.

Education Commission of the States. 2002. *Education That Lasts: How Service Learning Can Become an Integral Part of Schools, States, and Communities.* Denver, CO: Education Commission of the States.

This useful guide is designed for the broadest range of stake-holders—from state policymakers, administrators, and school board members to parents, teachers and students—to enable them to institutionalize service learning on the basis of vision, shared leadership, and self-interest. *On-line.*

Fullwood, P. Catlin. 2001. *The New Girls Movement: Implications for Youth Programs.* New York, NY: Collaborative Fund for Healthy Girls, Healthy Women, and Ms. Foundation for Women.

This report articulates core principles underlying the increasing number of projects for empowering girls and young women, both in their general efforts to contribute to their communities and in their specific attempts to address issues such as sexual harassment, violence, and media-mediated body images that can disable girls and young women from becoming effective citizens and "authors of their own lives." It testifies to the increasing convergence of feminist-inspired practice and the language of democracy and civic engagement. *On-line.*

Funders' Collaborative on Youth Organizing. 2003–2004. *Occasional Papers Series on Youth Organizing.* New York, NY: Funders' Collaborative on Youth Organizing.

This series provides insight into the burgeoning field of youth organizing as a combination of community organizing and youth development practices and distinguishes it from other forms of community service and youth civic engagement. *On-line.*

Garza, Pam and Pam Stevens. 2002. *Best Practices in Youth Philanthropy.* Austin, TX: Coalition of Community Foundations for Youth.

Published by CCFY, a coalition of 200 community foundations that has made youth civic engagement a centerpiece of its work, this clear guide draws from a decade of experience of youth decision making in formal grantmaking, which has grown to some 250 programs nationwide. It contains a guide to many other related resources. *On-line.*

Gibson, Cynthia and Peter Levine. 2003. *The Civic Mission of Schools.* New York, NY, and College Park, MD: Carnegie Corporation and CIRCLE: The Center for Information and Research on Civic Learning and Engagement.

This compelling report represents the consensus of some 60 leading practitioners, organizations, and researchers in the field of civic education about the need and potential for reinvigorating the civic mission of schools and has spurred this movement considerably. It also contains a detailed policy agenda for educational institutions and administrators, state and federal policymakers, researchers, funders, and colleges and universities engaged in teacher training. *On-line.*

Godwin, Tracy, with David J. Steinhart and Betsy A. Fulton. 1998. *Peer Justice and Youth Empowerment: An Implementation Guide for Teen Court Programs.* Lexington, KY: National Youth Court Center.

This is a detailed, hands-on guide to the various models of teen courts and how to establish and run them. It also provides a list of teen courts nationwide and various resources available to them.

Godwin, Tracy M. 2001. *The Role of Restorative Justice in Teen Courts: A Preliminary Look.* Lexington, KY: American Probation and Parole Association.

This analysis by the director of the National Youth Court Center examines the principles of restorative justice and ways to incorporate them into the practices of teen courts in the interests of enhanced community problem solving.

Innovation Center for Community and Youth Development and National 4-H Council. 2001. *Building Community: A Toolkit for Youth and Adults in Charting Assets and Creating Change.* Chevy Chase, MD: Innovation Center for Community and Youth Development and National 4-H Council.

Building on the work of the Innovation Center with communities in the 4-H system, this very usable guide contains a discussion of core principles for youth-adult partnerships, as well as practices for developing a vision, action plans, and strategies for sustainability.

Institute for Youth, Education, and Families, National League of Cities. N.d. *Promoting Youth Participation: Action Kit for Municipal Leaders.* Washington, DC: National League of Cities.

This convenient kit includes core principles, resources, and models, especially of citywide youth commissions and councils.

Irby, Merita, Thaddeus Ferber, and Karen Pittman, with Joel Tolman and Nicole Yohalem. 2001. *Youth Action: Youth Contributing to Communities, Communities Supporting Youth.* Community and Youth Development Series, volume 6. Takoma Park, MD: The Forum for Youth Investment, International Youth Foundation.

> This influential report provides an essential frame for "youth action" as a key component of youth development and maps a diversity of approaches and pathways. *On-line.*

Mullahey, Ramona, Yve Susskind, and Barry Checkoway. 1999. *Youth Participation in Community Planning.* American Planning Association, Planning Advisory Service, Report Number 486.

> This report presents core principle and practices of youth participation in planning activities.

National Commission on Service Learning. 2002. *Learning In Deed: The Power of Service Learning for America's Schools.* Battle Creek, MI and Columbus, OH: W.K. Kellogg Foundation and The John Glenn Institute for Public Service and Public Policy.

> Chaired by Senator John Glenn, the commission summarizes the research and key practices of service learning in K–12 schools and offers an important policy agenda for advancing it further. *On-line.*

National 4-H Council. 2002. *The National Conversation on Youth Development in the 21st Century: Final Report.* Chevy Chase, MD: National 4-H Council.

> Based on 1,640 local and state conversations among some 50,000 youth and adults throughout the 4-H system, marking its recent centennial, this report articulates a vision of "empowering youth as equal partners" and "equal citizens." It includes bold recommendations on how to do this in government, schools, community organizations, and private-sector initiatives. *On-line.*

Project 540. 2003. *"Students Turn for a Change."* Providence, RI: Rhode Island PBS.

> Filmed by high school students from around the country, this documentary provides stories of young people engaged in the civic life of schools and communities through a project involving 140,000 students in 230 schools in 15 states during 2002–2003.

————. 2004. *Students Turning into Citizens: Lessons Learned from Project 540.* Providence, RI: Providence College.

   This report examines the lessons of this two-year initiative to enhance participation through schoolwide and student-led dialogue and action.

Skelton, Nan, Harry Boyte, and Lynn Sordelet. 2002. *Youth Civic Engagement: Reflections on an Emerging Public Idea.* Minneapolis, MN: Center for Democracy and Citizenship.

   Drawing on more than a decade of experience in Public Achievement and other organizing projects among youth and adults, the authors argue for a conception of youth civic engagement that is based on the idea of citizens as cocreators of a common life, working collaboratively with others in a diverse community.

Study Circles Resource Center. 2003. *Organizing Study Circles with Young People: A Hands-On Guide for Youth and Adults.* Pomfret, CT: Study Circles Resource Center.

   This guide shows how young people can fully engage themselves in every aspect of organizing study circles in a wide range of formats in schools, youth groups, and in communitywide study circle programs. *On-line.*

Terry, John. 2002. *Community Youth Development Anthology 2002.* Sudbury, MA: Institute for Just Communities.

   This invaluable anthology from the CYD Journal presents key components of the CYD frame, as well as case studies of best practices and tools for evaluation. *On-line.*

Tolman, Joel, Karen Pittman, et al. 2001. *Youth Acts, Community Impacts: Stories of Youth Engagement with Real Results.* Community and Youth Development Series, volume 7. Takoma Park, MD: The Forum for Youth Investment, International Youth Foundation.

   Noting a convergence on youth action in a number of fields, including the broad community-building movement, this report presents eight case studies from the United States and around the world. American studies include The Food Project (Massachusetts), Lubec Aquaculture Project (Maine), Philadelphia Student Union (Pennsylvania), and Educational Video Center (New York). *On-line.*

YMCA of the USA. 2003. *YMCA Youth Civic Engagement Guide: Strategies and Tools for Increasing Civic Engagement.* Chicago, IL: YMCA of the USA.

> This excellent guide builds on existing practice in innovative local Y's, as well as on models in the broader civic renewal movement, to enable staff and youth to expand opportunities for civic engagement and promote institutional culture change in line with the civic mission of the YMCA. *On-line.*

YouthBuild USA. N.d. *Leadership Development at a YouthBuild Program.* Somerville, MA: YouthBuild USA.

> Based on more than a decade of experience, this guide provides YouthBuild programs with extensive resources for leadership development at every level of their work from on-the-job construction and classroom sites to policy committees, neighborhoods, media, and legislatures.

Youth Leadership Institute. 2001. *Changing the Face of Giving: An Assessment of Youth Philanthropy.* San Francisco, CA: James Irvine Foundation.

> This report examines the key purposes and components of the growing practice of youth philanthropy that engages youth directly in grantmaking to improve communities. *On-line.*

Zeldin, Shepherd, Annette Kusgen McDaniel, Dmitri Topitzes, and Matt Calvert. 2000. *Youth in Decision Making: A Study on the Impacts of Youth on Adults and Organizations.* Chevy Chase, MD: National 4-H Council/Innovation Center for Community and Youth Development.

> Based on a sample of 19 youth and 29 adults from 15 innovative youth organizations, this report examines the principles and practices of youth-adult partnerships and the ways in which organizations can change to provide youth a significant role in governance. *On-line.*

Healthy Communities

Adams, Christopher Freeman (ed.). 1998. *Voices from America: Ten Healthy Communities, Stories Across the Nation.* Chicago, IL: Hospital Research and Education Trust.

These stories profile ways in which communities can collaborate for health improvement and community development.

Ayre, Darvin, Gruffie Clough, and Tyler Norris. 2000. *Facilitating Community Change.* Boulder, CO: Community Initiatives.

Drawn from rich experience in facilitative leadership, healthy communities, and other models in what it calls the "community movement," this hands-on guide can be used in a broad range of settings. Especially useful are the checklists and graphics.

Bogue, Richard and Claude Hall, Jr. (eds.). 1997. *Health Network Innovations: How 20 Communities Are Improving Their Systems Through Collaboration.* Chicago, IL: American Hospital Publishing.

This collection provides valuable case descriptions from the Community Care Networks Demonstration Program, emphasizing innovative forms of collaboration among health care organizations and community groups.

CDC/ATSDR Committee on Community Engagement. 1997. *Principles of Community Engagement.* Atlanta, GA: Centers for Disease Control and Prevention, Public Health Practice Program Office.

Drawn from the CDC's PATCH model of community health planning, as well as assets-based community development and other participation models, this guide provides public health practitioners with principles to enable collaboration and community self-determination in health improvement efforts.

Duhl, Leonard and Peter Lee (eds.). 2000. *Focus on Healthy Communities, special double issue of Public Health Reports* 115: 2–3 (March/April and May/June).

Edited by two prominent leaders in the healthy communities movement, this special issue includes important articles reviewing core concepts and practices, as well as the history of the movement.

Durch, Jane S., Linda A. Bailey, and Michael A. Stoto (eds.). 1997. *Improving Health in the Community: A Role for Performance Monitoring.* Washington, DC: National Academy Press.

>   Based on a broad understanding of health, this important publication by the Institute of Medicine at the National Academy of Sciences provides tools for community health coalitions to engage in a collaborative community health improvement process that uses population-based performance monitoring to achieve accountability for action.

Gunderson, Gary. 1997. *Deeply Woven Roots: Improving the Quality of Life in Your Community.* Minneapolis, MN: Fortress Press.

>   Drawing on the networks of the Interfaith Health Program, the author provides a relational and assets-based approach to health ministries in faith communities designed for lay leaders and clergy alike.

Johnson, Kathryn, Wynne Grossman, and Anne Cassidy (eds.). 1996. *Collaborating to Improve Community Health: Workbook and Guide to Best Practices in Creating Healthier Communities and Populations.* San Francisco, CA: Jossey-Bass.

>   Drawn from the experiences of several dozen innovative organizations, this early and important guide provides practical insight on convening community stakeholders, developing a healthy communities vision, planning for action, and monitoring progress.

Lasker, Roz D. and Elisa S. Weiss. 2003. "Broadening Participation in Community Problem Solving: A Multidisciplinary Model to Support Collaborative Practice and Research," *Journal of Urban Health: Bulletin of the New York Academy of Medicine* 80:1 (March), 14–60.

>   Using the experience of nine community partnerships in the Turning Point initiative, the authors develop a model of "community health governance" for broadly participatory collaborative processes and complex problem solving to improve community health.

Seifer, Serena and Rachel Vaughn. 2004. *Community-Campus Partnerships for Health: Making a Positive Impact.* Battle Creek, MI: W.K. Kellogg Foundation. *On-line.*

This report explores lessons of partnerships between campuses and communities in 13 Community Voices sites, with special emphasis on service learning, community health worker development, and diversity.

Solari-Twadell, Phyllis and Mary Ann McDermott (eds.). 1999. *Parish Nursing: Promoting Whole Person Health Within Faith Communities.* Thousand Oaks, CA: Sage.

Bringing together leading practitioners and academics, this collection provides a handbook of the theory and practice of parish nursing as a form of health promotion and health ministry within faith communities.

Wolff, Tom. 2003. "The Healthy Communities Movement: A Time for Transformation." *National Civic Review* 92:2 (Summer), 95–111.

The founder of Healthy Communities Massachusetts reflects on some of the problems that have led to the recent stagnation of the healthy communities movement, including the diffuse nature of goals and the difficulty community actors have had in persuading health institutions to buy into robust and empowering civic models and broad conceptions of health.

Public Journalism and Civic Communications

Bollier, David, and Tim Watts. 2002. *Saving the Information Commons: A New Public Interest Agenda in Digital Media.* Washington, DC: New America Foundation.

A comprehensive overview of the information commons movement with practical ideas and information resources.

Center for Digital Democracy. N.d. *A Citizen's Guide to Digital Democracy.* On-line at www.democraticmedia.org.

The site presents a guide to broadband as commons resources, with accompanying "dot.commons tour."

Friedland, Lewis A., and Harry Boyte. 2000. *The New Information Commons: Community Information Partnerships and Civic Change.* Minneapolis, MN: Center for Democracy and Citizenship.

An early statement linking the larger idea of the information commons to the needs of local communities for new public spaces.

Gibbs, Cheryl K., and Tom Warhover. 2002. *Getting the Whole Story: Reporting and Writing the News.* New York, NY: Guilford Press.
This is the only comprehensive textbook on reporting the news from a public and civic journalism perspective.

Harwood, Richard C. and John McCrehan. 2000. *Tapping Civic Life: How to Report First, and Best, What's Happening in Your Community.* Second Edition. Washington, DC, and College Park, MD: Pew Center for Civic Journalism and J-Lab.
One of the best short manuals on community-based reporting and mapping from a civic perspective. The book includes many useful and practical reporting techniques. *On-line.*

Merritt, Davis. 1998. *Public Journalism and Public Life: Why Telling the News Is Not Enough.* Hillsdale, NJ: Lawrence Erlbaum.
One of the founders of the public journalism movement issues both a call to action and a statement of basic principles.

Schaffer, Jan and Edward D. Miller. 1995. *Civic Journalism: Six Case Studies.* Washington, DC: Pew Center for Civic Journalism.
This report provides valuable case studies from the early years of the movement. *On-line.*

Scholarly Studies

Civic Renewal and Democracy

American Political Science Association, Standing Committee on Civic Education and Engagement. 2004. *Democracy at Risk: Renewing the Political Science of Citizenship.* Washington, DC: APSA.

This wide-ranging report presents an indispensable overview of political science literature on the decline of civic engagement and the continuing challenges, with a focus on three areas: electoral processes, urban metropolises, and nonprofit and voluntary sectors. It also offers useful guidelines for thinking about reform, as well as the needs of future research.

Barber, Benjamin. 1984. *Strong Democracy.* Berkeley, CA: University of California Press.

This important theoretical work develops a compelling case for a strong version of democratic deliberation and engagement by ordinary citizens, rather than just by elected representatives. It has profoundly influenced many civic innovators over the past two decades.

Bellah, Robert, Richard Madsen, William Sullivan, Ann Swidler, and Steven Tipton. 1991. *The Good Society.* New York, NY: Knopf.

Building on arguments in their now-classic *Habits of the Heart*, the authors sketch the contours of a society and polity based on strong community and democratic values.

Berger, Peter L. and Richard John Neuhaus. 1996. *To Empower People: From State to Civil Society.* Twentieth Anniversary Edition, Michael Novak (ed.). Washington, DC: American Enterprise Institute Press.

Berger and Neuhaus's original text on "mediating structures" is reissued with accompanying essays, largely from "civic conservatives," although its influence has extended across the political spectrum. Berger and Neuhaus respond.

Berry, Jeffrey M. 1999. *The New Liberalism: The Rising Power of Citizen Groups.* Washington, DC: Brookings Institution.

This study examines citizen lobbying groups as a major force for democratic politics and agenda setting in recent decades.

Boyte, Harry. 2004. *Everyday Politics.* Philadelphia, PA: University of Pennsylvania Press.

Building on a series of works that have helped define a new civic populism (Free Spaces, Commonwealth, Building America), Boyte extends the insights from innovative practice at the Center for Democracy and Citizenship and argues for a "commonwealth of freedom" in which ordinary citizens, working with civic professionals in many kinds of institutions, become cocreators of democracy.

Cohen, Jean and Andrew Arato. 1992. *Civil Society and Political Theory.* New York, NY: Cambridge University Press.

This is a formative theoretical work on the idea of civil society, written largely in the critical theory tradition.

Crenson, Matthew A. and Benjamin Ginsberg. 2002. *Downsizing Democracy: How America Sidelined Its Citizens and Privatized Its Public.* Baltimore, MD: Johns Hopkins University Press.

The authors analyze how an older ideal of the collective citizenry has given way to a concept of personal, autonomous democracy in which political change is effected through litigation and lobbying rather than active participation.

Dorf, Michael and Charles Sabel. 1998. "A Constitution of Democratic Experimentalism," *Columbia Law Review* 98:2 (March 1998), 267–473.

The authors examine how the administrative state can shift to promote civic empowerment and stakeholder involvement.

Eberly, Don E. (ed.) 1998. *America's Promise: Civil Society and the Renewal of American Culture.* Lanham, MD: Rowman and Littlefield.

Edited by a leading civic conservative, this collection of essays on the role of civil society in civic renewal ranges across the political spectrum.

Fishkin, James. 1995. *The Voice of the People: Public Opinion and Democracy.* New Haven, CT: Yale University Press.

    The author makes an important theoretical case for deliberative democracy and develops an innovative model of "deliberative polling" as an alternative to the usual public opinion research.

Fung, Archon and Erik Olin Wright (eds.). 2003. *Deepening Democracy: Institutional Innovations in Empowered Participatory Governance.* London: Verso.

    This excellent collection centers on four case studies of "empowered participatory governance" around the world (including community policing and local school committees in Chicago and habitat conservations plans across the United States), accompanied by critical discussion, by a broad group of scholars, of institutional design.

Gastil, John. 2000. *By Popular Demand: Revitalizing Representative Democracy Through Deliberative Elections.* Berkeley, CA: University of California Press.

    This astute study examines the limits of representation as a vehicle of public voice and, drawing on a variety of current innovations in deliberative dialogue, develops a proposal for citizen panels.

Harwood Group. 1991. *Citizens and Politics.* Dayton, OH: Kettering Foundation.

    This influential critical and early study in framing the civic renewal debate shows that citizens are not apathetic but quite angry at how professionals have pushed them out of politics and displaced them from their rightful role in governing the nation.

Ingram, Helen and Steven Rathgeb Smith (eds.). 1993. *Public Policy for Democracy.* Washington, DC: Brookings Institution.

    This important collection of essays examines both general principles and specific cases for designing policy and administration to support citizen deliberation and problem solving.

Ladd, Everett Carll. 1999. *The Ladd Report.* New York, NY: Free Press.

    Extensive public opinion research is marshaled to counter the argument that civic life in the United States has been declining.

Levine, Peter. 2000. *The New Progressive Era: Towards a Fair and Deliberative Democracy.* Lanham, MD: Rowman and Littlefield.

Written by a leading figure in various national projects of the civic renewal movement, this book provides important diagnoses of our democratic distemper and develops a series of interrelated reform proposals for government, schools, foundations, the press, and other institutions.

Mathews, David. 1999. *Politics for People: Finding a Responsible Public Voice.* Second edition. Urbana, IL: University of Illinois Press.

Drawing from both the history of democratic theory and public opinion research, Mathews elaborates a clear and powerful role for citizens in public deliberation and problem solving and shows how this can complement the role of elected and appointed officials.

Morse, Suzanne W. 2004. *Smart Communities: How Citizens and Local Leaders Can Use Strategic Thinking to Build a Brighter Future.* California: Jossey-Bass.

Based on ten years of research by the Pew Partnership for Change, the author highlights 14 communities that achieved success using strategic decision making. Seven "leverage points" are featured as promoting "smart" community planning.

Norris, Pippa. 2002. *Democratic Phoenix: Reinventing Political Activism.* New York, NY: Cambridge University Press.

Using data from 200 countries, the author argues that political participation has not decreased and that the thesis of civic decline is overdrawn even for the United States, with the reinvention of civic activism coming largely from new social movements, protest, and the Internet.

PEGS. *The Good Society.* College Park, MD: Department of Government and Politics.

This journal provides indispensable theoretical discussion of questions of democracy, public life, and civic empowerment.

Putnam, Robert. 2000. *Bowling Alone: The Collapse and Revival of American Community.* New York, NY: Simon and Schuster.

This book provides the most extensive data on aggregate levels of social capital and makes a compelling case that these have declined in recent years, especially as a result of generational changes and television, with further factors of sprawl and the increasing participation of women in the workforce.

Putnam, Robert D. and Lewis M. Feldstein, with Don Cohen. 2003. *Better Together: Restoring the American Community.* New York: Simon and Schuster.

Prompted by the growing literature on civic innovation in the United States, Putnam and his colleagues turn their attention to 12 case studies that range from neighborhood associations and assets-based community development to youth service and union organizing. The authors present very readable and useful portraits.

Sandel, Michael. 1996. *Democracy's Discontent: America in Search of a Public Philosophy.* Cambridge, MA: Harvard University Press.

This sweeping historical and theoretical treatise examines the defects in our governing philosophy that disable both Democrats and Republicans. The author offers an alternative governing philosophy built on self-government and a "political economy of citizenship."

Schneider, Anne Larason and Helen Ingram. 1997. *Policy Design for Democracy.* Lawrence, KS: University Press of Kansas.

The authors elaborate an important set of principles to enable policy to enhance active civic engagement rather than displace it. The book is especially helpful on the social construction of target populations in policy design.

Schudson, Michael. *The Good Citizen: A History of American Civic Life.* New York, NY: Free Press.

The author provides a provocative analysis of several distinct eras in the history of American citizenship and argues that the rights revolution, while posing problems, has done more to enhance democracy than to endanger it. He also makes a good case for being realistic about what we can expect of participation, without closing off expanded roles for citizens in public problem solving and collaboration with professionals.

Sirianni, Carmen and Lewis A. Friedland. 2001. *Civic Innovation in America: Community Empowerment, Public Policy, and the Movement for Civic Renewal.* Berkeley, CA: University of California Press.

This book examines civic innovation as an extended social learning process over several decades in four arenas (urban, environment, health, and journalism) and presents the first scholarly analysis of the emergence of a civic renewal movement.

Skocpol, Theda. 2003. *Diminished Democracy: From Membership to Management in American Civic Life.* Norman, OK: University of Oklahoma Press.

This book examines the development of multitiered civic associations in American history and their decline in the past half-century. Her remedy for civic decline is to find ways of reinventing local, broad-based organizing linked to national advocacy.

Sullivan, William M. 1995. *Work and Integrity: The Crisis and Promise of Professionalism in America.* New York, NY: Harper Business.

Drawing on a historical and philosophical critique of professional work as a narrow technique and self-serving career, the author develops the notion of "civic professionalism" as work with broad public purpose linked to democratic practice.

Warren, Mark E. 2001. *Democracy and Association.* Princeton, NJ: Princeton University Press.

The author provides a systematic theoretical analysis of the relation between association and democracy in a world characterized by institutional differentiation, social complexity, and the pluralization and reflexivity of individual choices and cultural identities. A fundamental work for thinking about how "plural" the venues of politics and associational niches have become and what a "democratic ecology of associations" might look like.

Warren, Mark E. (ed.). 1999. *Democracy and Trust.* New York, NY: Cambridge University Press.

This valuable collection of theoretical essays examines the ways in which both trust and distrust are essential to democratic representation, civic collaboration, and popular resistance.

Yankelovich, Daniel. 1991. *Coming to Public Judgment: Making Democracy Work in a Complex World.* Syracuse, NY: Syracuse University Press.

Based on years of public opinion research, the author examines the difference between mass opinion, often manipulated by experts, and a genuine democratic process of citizens coming to public judgment.

Social Movement Theory

Benford, Robert D. and David A. Snow. 2000. "Framing Processes and Social Movements: An Overview and Assessment," *Annual Review of Sociology* 26: 611–39.

    This essential literature review discusses the key conceptual issues in social movement framing.

Davis, Joseph E. (ed.). 2002. *Stories of Change: Narrative and Social Movements*. Albany, NY: State University of New York Press.

    This collection examines the critical role of storytelling, or "bundles of narratives" in movements.

Della Porta, Donatella and Mario Diani. 1999. *Social Movements: An Introduction*. Malden, MA: Blackwell.

    This book offers an insightful and relatively comprehensive overview of the literature in the field.

Diani, Mario and Doug McAdam (eds.). *Social Movements and Networks: Relational Approaches to Collective Action*. New York, NY: Oxford University Press.

    This collection of essays examines both conceptual and methodological issues of network analysis for understanding social movements in a wide range of times and places.

Gamson, William, Bruce Fireman, and Steven Rytina. 1982. *Encounters with Unjust Authority*. Homewood, IL: Dorsey.

    This essential work examines injustice frames and the practices of micromobilization against unjust authorities.

Giugni, Mario G., Doug McAdam, and Charles Tilly (eds.). 1998. *From Contention to Democracy*. Lanham, MD: Rowman and Littlefield.

    These essays explore the relationship of social movements to political and social change and especially to processes of democratization.

Goodwin, Jeff and James M. Jasper (eds.). 2004. *Rethinking Social Movements: Structure, Meaning, and Emotion*. Lanham, MD: Rowman and Littlefield.

This collection examines some of the core issues distinguishing the dominant, structural approach from the cultural or constructivist tradition in social movement theorizing.

Johnston, Hank and Bert Klandermans (eds.). 1995. *Social Movements and Culture*. Minneapolis, MN: University of Minnesota Press.
These essays examine key issues of culture, narrative, identity, and frame in social movements.

Meyer, David S. and Sidney Tarrow (eds.). 1998. *The Social Movement Society*. Lanham, MD: Rowman and Littlefield.
This collection explores how movements pervade many areas of institutional life, culture, and policy.

Meyer, David S., Nancy Whittier, and Belinda Robnett (eds.). 2002. *Social Movements: Identity, Culture, and the State*. New York, NY: Oxford University Press.
This collection offers valuable rethinking of the dynamics and diversity of movement culture and identity in various well-known American movements, as well as some lesser-known comparative cases.

Morris, Aldon D. and Carol McClurg Mueller (eds.). 1992. *Frontiers in Social Movement Theory*. New Haven, CT: Yale University Press.
These essays include important analyses of social movement master frames, collective identities, and consensus and conflict movements, among other topics.

Polletta, Francesca. 2002. *Freedom Is an Endless Meeting: Democracy in American Social Movements*. Chicago, IL: University of Chicago Press.
This wonderful book provides a sweeping reinterpretation of movements in the United States over the course of the twentieth century in terms of various models of "participatory democracy" and its innovatory, developmental, and strategic benefits, as well as its limits.

Ronchon, Thomas R. 2000. *Culture Moves: Ideas, Activism, and Changing Values*. Princeton, NJ: Princeton University Press.
This book analyzes the processes of cultural transformation by which small communities of critical thinkers develop new ideas and disseminate them through larger social movements.

Tarrow, Sidney. 1998. *Power in Movement: Social Movements and Contentious Politics.* Second edition. New York, NY: Cambridge University Press.

   This is a classic study of contention as action repertoires, broad cycles of protest, a political strategy, and the power of social movements to effect change.

Community Organizing and Community Development

Berry, Jeffrey, Kent Portney, and Ken Thomson. 1993. *The Rebirth of Urban Democracy.* Washington, DC: Brookings Institution.

   Though models of neighborhood governance have continued to evolve considerably since the research for this book was conducted, this work provides the most extensive comparative and quantitative study of cities with formal systems of neighborhood governance, along with data from a broader sample of cities and projects. It grounds the empirical analysis in a sophisticated discussion of participatory democratic theory throughout.

Bookman, Ann. 2004. *Starting in Our Own Backyards: How Working Families Can Build Community and Survive the New Economy.* New York, NY: Routledge.

   Based on close observation of 40 biotechnology employees and their families, this important book analyzes the new forms of community that are emerging to enable creative solutions to the challenges of combining family, work, and civic life. The author, who highlights the role of women in community care work, sees these formal and informal innovations as part of the broad civic renewal movement.

Ferguson, Ronald and William Dickens (eds.). 1999. *Urban Problems and Community Development.* Washington, DC: Brookings Institution.

   This collection of essays analyzes a broad range of dimensions of community development as part of a single, broad-based movement with a vision to build the assets of communities, including physical, human, social, financial, and political capital. It is a superb overall map of the field and its challenges.

Forester, John. 1999. *The Deliberative Practitioner.* Cambridge, MA: MIT Press.

    Through rich case studies, a leading planning theorist examines how planners can facilitate deliberative democracy in their professional practice, even in the face of conflict, power, and inequality.

Fung, Archon. 2004. *Empowered Participation: Reinventing Urban Democracy.* Princeton, NJ: Princeton University Press.

    Based on extensive citywide data and six in-depth case studies, this superb study examines the democratic transformations that become possible with good policy design of community policing and local school councils that engage residents, civic organizations, police, parents, teachers, and principals in collaborative work to improve schools and neighborhood safety. "Accountable autonomy" combines decentralized initiative with support from and accountability to the city's central police and school authorities. This model of empowered, pragmatic participation holds up well against various theoretical arguments against deliberative democracy.

Hart, Stephen. 2001. *Cultural Dilemmas of Progressive Politics: Styles of Engagement among Grassroots Activists.* Chicago, IL: University of Chicago Press.

    This book examines the cultural dimensions of several kinds of grassroots groups, including faith-based community organizations, and argues for the importance of a broad vision of social justice and human rights.

Johnson, Steven. Forthcoming. *Civic Portland: Transformation and Renewal in an American City, 1960–1999.* Columbus, OH: Ohio State University Press.

    This comprehensive 40-year inventory of civic organizations and selected case studies of innovation in Portland, Oregon, convincingly demonstrates how dynamic, inclusive, and positive civic change can accompany the decline in traditional civic organizations at the city level.

Karp, David R. (ed.). 1998. *Community Justice: An Emerging Field.* Lanham, MD: Rowman and Littlefield.

    This collection of essays addresses a variety of dimensions of what the editor characterizes as the "community justice movement."

Kelling, George L. and Catherine M. Coles. 1996. *Fixing Broken Windows: Restoring Order and Reducing Crime in Our Communities.* New York, NY: Free Press.

    Building on an earlier influential article that highlighted the importance of responding to lesser forms of community disorder, the authors develop a more extensive critique of professional policing removed from the life of communities.

Light, Paul C. 1998. *Sustaining Innovation: Creating Nonprofit and Government Organizations That Innovate Naturally.* San Francisco, CA: Jossey-Bass.

    Based on a study of 26 nonprofit and government organizations, the author examines how organizations can innovate for the public good and engage citizens in genuine public work, rather than treating them as "customers" or "clients."

McRoberts, Omar M. 2003. *Streets of Glory: Church and Community in a Black Urban Neighborhood.* Chicago, IL: University of Chicago Press.

    This study of Four Corners in Boston analyzes the mismatch between some activist African American churches, whose membership is often drawn from outside the neighborhood, and locally focused revitalization strategies. It also cautions against placing too much hope in faith-based social welfare programs promoted through federal policies such as Charitable Choice.

Medoff, Peter and Holly Sklar. 1994. *Streets of Hope: The Fall and Rise of an Urban Neighborhood.* Boston, MA: South End Press.

    This book tells the story of the rebirth of an inner-city neighborhood in Boston through the Dudley Street Neighborhood Initiative, which combines multiracial community organizing with assets-based community development. A companion PBS documentary, "Holding Ground," is also available.

Miller, Susan L. 1999. *Gender and Community Policing: Walking the Talk.* Boston, MA: Northeastern University Press.

    This book provides a close-up look at the everyday work of community police officers in a midwestern city and analyzes some of the gendered styles of such work.

Oliver, J. Eric. 2001. *Democracy in Suburbia.* Princeton, NJ: Princeton University Press.

The author examines the unfortunate impacts of urban/suburban segmentation on civic capacities and advocates that we "remake the democratic metropolis" by combining the virtues of local and metropolitan forms of government and engagement.

Osterman, Paul. 2002. *Gathering Power: The Future of Progressive Politics in America*. Boston, MA: Beacon.

This study of faith-based organizing, largely by the Texas IAF, is especially useful for its job training and other economic strategies and makes the case for such local organizing as the foundation for a larger progressive coalition, including unions and other groups.

Roberts and Kay, Inc. 2000. *Toward Competent Communities: Best Practices for Producing Community-wide Study Circles*. Lexington, KY: RKI.

This two-year evaluation examines 17 demonstrated sites of excellence to cull lessons of best practices in study circles programs. It gives special emphasis to dialogues on race. *On-line*.

Roth, Jeffrey A. (ed.). 2000. *National Evaluation of the COPS Program—Title I of the 1994 Crime Act*. Washington, DC: National Institute of Justice.

This collection explores the spread and impact of community policing practices across the nation, which resulted from the $9 billion of federal grants to state, local, and other public law enforcement agencies by the Office of Community-Oriented Policing Services in the latter half of the 1990s.

Schorr, Lisbeth. 1997. *Common Purpose: Strengthening Families and Neighborhoods to Rebuild America*. New York, NY: Anchor.

This book develops a compelling analysis of the limits of bureaucratic and categorical approaches to human service delivery and shows how an outcomes-based approach can engage families, communities, nonprofits, and public agencies in innovative partnerships.

Shirley, Dennis. 1997. *Community Organizing for Urban School Reform*. Austin, TX: University of Texas Press.

This book presents the model of congregation-based organizing and social capital development of the Texas IAF and masterfully analyzes its school reform efforts at the individual school, city, and state levels.

Shirley, Dennis. 2002. *Valley Interfaith and School Reform*. Austin, TX: University of Texas Press.

> Following up on his earlier study, Shirley examines school reform through faith-based organizing in the Rio Grande Valley, with a detailed focus on three schools as vibrant "laboratories of democracy."

Skogan, Wesley and Susan Hartnett. 1997. *Community Policing, Chicago Style*. New York: Oxford University Press.

> In this important study of the early phases of community policing in Chicago (which has been updated through ongoing evaluations), the authors present an in-depth analysis of changes in institutional and professional police practice, as well as participation of citizens through community groups, beat meetings, and district advisory committees. They also articulate especially clearly the four broad principles of community policing.

Skogan, Wesley, Susan Hartnett, Jill DuBois, et al. 2000. *Public Involvement: Community Policing in Chicago*. Washington, DC: National Institute of Justice.

> Based on observation of more than 450 beat meetings over a three-year period, this study finds relatively high attendance and identifies key factors in determining awareness, participation, and satisfaction with the new role of the police.

Skogan, Wesley (ed.). 2003. *Community Policing: Can It Work?* Belmont, CA: Wadsworth.

> This extensive overview of the field includes a wide range of perspectives on the successes and limits of community policing, as well as the great variation in practice, but clearly demonstrates that the community policing movement has profoundly impacted professional practice and the discourse of local governance.

Smock, Kristina. 2004. *Democracy in Action: Community Organizing and Urban Change*. New York, NY: Columbia University Press.

> Drawing on eight case studies in Chicago and two secondary ones in Portland, Oregon, the author analyzes five general models of contemporary urban organizing: power-based, community-building, civic, women-centered, and transformative.

Stone, Clarence N., Jeffrey R. Henig, Bryan D. Jones, and Carol Pierannunzi. 2001. *Building Civic Capacity: The Politics of Reforming Urban Schools.* Lawrence, KS: University Press of Kansas.

Following an ambitious 11 city study funded by the National Science Foundation, the authors argue that genuine school reform depends on developing a common vision and civic partnerships across a broad spectrum of civic, business, and government organizations and sectors of the community. The book offers invaluable insight into how civic coalitions can be built from above and below.

Thomson, Ken. 2001. *From Neighborhood to Nation: The Democratic Foundations of Civil Society.* Lebanon, NH: University Press of New England.

Drawing from the research of an earlier Tufts University study of neighborhood associations (for which he was a coinvestigator), the author provides further analysis of institutional design, as well as measures of the extent of organization and effectiveness in the political process.

Warren, Mark R. 2001. *Dry Bones Rattling: Community Building to Revitalize American Democracy.* Princeton, NJ: Princeton University Press.

This is a rich and comprehensive account of the Texas IAF's congregation-based organizing practices, policies, and strategies to revitalize communities and build social capital. It includes an especially interesting account of leadership development and democracy, as well as the challenges of multiracial organizing.

Warren, Mark R. and Richard L. Wood. 2001. *Faith-Based Community Organizing: The State of the Field.* Jericho, NY: Interfaith Funders.

Drawn from a broad survey of local organizations in all the major networks, this report presents an overview of the entire field of faith-based community organizing and its growth. It is especially insightful on organizers' own strategic self-assessments.

Williamson, Thad, David Imbroscio, and Gar Alperovitz. 2002. *Making a Place for Community: Local Democracy in a Global Era.* New York, NY: Routledge.

This book locates democratic community strategies in the larger context of globalization, free trade, and urban sprawl and develops a policy agenda to stabilize geographic communities economically. It contains an excellent appendix on "resources for rebuilding."

Wood, Richard L. 2002. *Faith in Action: Religion, Race, and Democratic Organizing in America.* Chicago, IL: University of Chicago Press.

This is an exceptionally rich account of faith-based organizing and its ethos of "ethical democracy" in the PICO national network, with a special focus on the city of Oakland. The author develops an astute comparison with race-based organizing in the same city and convincingly argues that faith-based organizing represents a movement, despite its aversion to movement language.

Wright, David J. 2001. *It Takes a Neighborhood: Strategies to Prevent Urban Decline. Albany,* NY: Rockefeller Institute Press.

The author examines a series of largely successful cases of comprehensive community initiatives to preserve and revitalize working-class neighborhoods in cities that participated in the Pew Charitable Trusts' Neighborhood Preservation Initiative.

Zhao, Jihong, Quint Thurman, and Nicholas Lovrich. 1995. "Community-Oriented Policing Across the United States: Factors and Impediments to Implementation." *American Journal of Police* 14, 11–28.

Among the impediments to community policing, the authors find not only the limited collaboration of other agencies (as of the mid-1990s), but also citizens' own pressures on police for immediate results over longer-term problem solving.

Civic Renewal and Democracy

Ahronowitz, Iris S. 2003. *Rooting the Community, Growing the Future: Two Massachusetts Urban Agriculture Organizations and Their Social Impacts.* Honors thesis. Cambridge, MA: Harvard University, Committee on Degrees in Social Studies.

The author explores the "urban agriculture movement" as a variant of other civic environmental movements, as well as the community youth development movement in these two cases (The Food Project and Nuestras Raíces), through which young people are engaged in innovative ways. *On-line.*

Baker, Mark and Jonathan Kusel. 2004. *Community Forestry in the United States: Learning from the Past, Creating the Future.* Washington, DC: Island Press.

Based on dozens of interviews and several regional workshops with key leaders in the Northeast, Intermountain West, and Pacific West, this book analyzes the emergence of a "community forestry movement" that enfranchises communities and workers in developing alternative resource stewardship strategies and considers how to nurture this movement in the coming years. The authors clearly recognize community forestry as a "sister movement" to other civic, community-building, and community-based environmental movements and its important role in broad civic renewal.

Cole, Luke W. and Sheila R. Foster. 2000. *From the Ground Up: Environmental Racism and the Rise of the Environmental Justice Movement.* New York, NY: New York University Press.

This book examines the emergence of the movement, especially in response to the siting of hazardous waste facilities in communities of color, and poses larger questions of the political economy of environmental racism and structures for public participation.

Cortner, Hanna and Margaret Moote. 1999. *The Politics of Ecosystem Management.* Washington, DC: Island Press.

The authors make a compelling argument that ecosystem management represents a profound paradigm shift in wrestling with complex and dynamic systems and that this shift requires innovative civic engagement and collaborative problem solving.

Donahue, Brian. 1999. *Reclaiming the Commons: Community Farms and Forests in a New England Town.* New Haven, CT: Yale University Press.

This engaging account by an environmental historian and founding member of Land's Sake in the Boston suburb of Weston, Massachusetts, provides indispensable insight into how citizens, working with their conservation commission, can protect common land and pursue sustainable agriculture and forestry on community farms. The book contains an important component of a civic environmental education strategy for youth.

Foreman, Christopher, Jr. 1999. *The Promise and Peril of Environmental Justice.* Washington, DC: Brookings Institution.

The author examines not only the contributions of the environmental justice approach, but also its policy and movement-building conundrums. He offers alternative ways of thinking about the movement's convergence with "livable communities," "stewardship," and "preservation" in the broader environmental movement.

Gobster, Paul H. and R. Bruce Hall (eds.). 2000. *Restoring Nature: Perspectives from the Social Sciences and Humanities.* Washington, DC: Island Press.

This excellent collection analyzes the civic controversy that emerged in the wake of the grassroots restoration work of the Volunteer Stewardship Network and Chicago Wilderness as other citizens challenged what it means to "restore nature" and questioned the science as well as the costs (to existing trees, wildlife, amenities, and public budgets). The essays provide insight into restoration volunteers' experiences but also challenge the growing national movement to develop a richer democratic practice.

Hershkowitz, Allen. 2002. *Bronx Ecology: Blueprint for a New Environmentalism.* Washington, DC: Island Press.

This study examines a pioneering attempt to apply industrial ecology to the design of the Bronx Community Paper Corporation and to develop local partnerships in the interest of sustainable economic development and social equity. While the ten-year effort ultimately failed, it began an important learning process for community-based entrepreneurial environmentalism.

John, DeWitt. 1994. *Civic Environmentalism: Alternatives to Regulation in States and Communities.* Washington, DC: Congressional Quarterly Press.

This book, which investigates a range of "horizontal learning communities" engaged in innovation, coined the term "civic environmentalism," and the author subsequently brought many of its lessons to the National Academy of Public Administration's efforts to reinvent environmental regulation at the EPA.

Kusel, Jonathan and Elisa Adler (eds.). 2003. *Forest Communities, Community Forests.* Lanham, MD: Rowman and Littlefield.

This essential collection, based on 12 case studies from every region in the country, explores the dynamics of forest management at local, state, and federal levels that take community and civic collaboration seriously.

Lichterman, Paul. 1996. *The Search for Political Community: American Activists Reinventing Commitment.* New York, NY: Cambridge University Press.

Based on a comparison of groups with diverse income and racial composition, this book examines the ways in which personalized commitment among local environmental activists can go hand in hand with community work for the public good.

Mazmanian, Daniel A. and Michael E. Kraft (eds). 1999. *Toward Sustainable Communities: Transition and Transformation in Environmental Policy.* Cambridge, MA: MIT Press.

This collection of essays explores three epochs in the environmental movement, with emphasis on the recent shift to community sustainability and case studies covering a range of policy areas.

Pellow, David and Robert Brulle (eds.). Forthcoming. *People, Power, and Pollution: A Critical Appraisal of the Environmental Justice Movement.* Cambridge, MA: MIT Press.

This collection of essays examines the environmental justice movement from a variety of angles, including the recent shift toward collaborative models for achieving healthy communities.

Portney, Kent E. 2003. *Taking Sustainable Cities Seriously: Economic Development, the Environment, and Quality of Life in American Cities.* Cambridge, MA: MIT Press.

This book analyzes the sustainable cities movement in the United States and explores some knotty analytic problems, including the role of citizen participation in the various models.

Press, Daniel. 2002. *Saving Open Space: The Politics of Local Preservation in California.* Berkeley, CA: University of California Press.

This study examines the local land conservation movement as a form of civic environmentalism and analyzes its collaboration with local and state government.

————. 1994. *Democratic Dilemmas in the Age of Ecology: Trees and Toxics in the American West.* Durham, NC: Duke University Press.
This book analyzes the centralization/decentralization debate in two arenas of environmental policy and makes a compelling case for greater democracy.

Roberts, J. Timmons and Melissa M. Toffolon-Weiss. 2001. *Chronicles from the Environmental Justice Frontline.* New York, NY: Cambridge University Press.
This book examines local struggles for environmental justice at the epicenter of the movement in Louisiana.

Shutkin, William. 2000. *The Land That Could Be: Environmentalism and Democracy in the Twenty-First Century.* Cambridge, MA: MIT Press.
This book represents the most ambitious attempt to theorize the civic dimensions of innovative environmental action today and includes four case studies of community-based conservation, smart growth, neighborhood revitalization, and urban agriculture, including that of the Dudley Street Neighborhood Initiative.

U.S. Environmental Protection Agency. 2003. *Evaluation of Community-Based Environmental Protection Projects: Accomplishments and Lessons Learned.* Washington, DC: U.S. EPA, Office of Policy Economics and Innovation.
This evaluation, conducted for the National Center for Environmental Innovation by Industrial Economics, Inc., focuses on five diverse community-based projects involving EPA regions. It finds significant capacity building, public legitimacy, and partnership benefits of the CBEP approach and delineates specific niche roles for EPA in furthering such work at the community level.

Weber, Edward P. 2003. *Bringing Society Back In: Grassroots Ecosystem Management, Accountability, and Sustainable Communities.* Cambridge, MA: MIT Press.
This analytically indispensable study of the GREM movement, which estimates its scope at 500 communities in the West, provides

three extended case studies and a rigorous (and generally very positive) test of whether such collaborative forms of resource governance can meet the standards of democratic accountability.

Engaged Campus

Bringle, Robert G., Richard Games, and Edward A. Malloy (eds.). 1999. *Colleges and Universities as Citizens*. Needham Heights, MA: Allyn & Bacon.

This important collection of essays examines pedagogical and institutional strategies for transforming universities into key civic actors.

Colby, Anne, Thomas Ehrlich, Elizabeth Beaumont, and Jason Stephens. 2003. *Educating Citizens: Preparing America's Undergraduates for Lives of Moral and Civic Responsibility*. San Francisco, CA: Jossey-Bass.

Written by a team of researchers at the Carnegie Foundation for the Advancement of Teaching, this excellent book provides an overview of several broad approaches ("community connections," "social justice," and "moral and civic virtue"), as well as extensive analysis of civic curricular and extracurricular activities and faculty and administrative leadership strategies. Rich examples from 12 core case-study campuses, as well as others, are woven throughout the text.

Ehrlich, Thomas (ed.). 2000. *Civic Responsibility and Higher Education*. Phoenix, AZ: Oryx Press.

This indispensable collection of essays examines broad issues about the democratic history, mission, and institutional capacities of higher education. It includes case studies from different kinds of institutions and discusses the emergence of this movement for civic renewal.

Eyler, Janet and Dwight E. Giles, Jr. 1999. *Where's the Learning in Service Learning?* San Francisco, CA: Jossey-Bass.

Based on national survey and interview data, this indispensable book examines what makes for good learning in service-learning courses.

Furco, Andrew and Shelley H. Billig (eds.). 2002. *Service Learning: The Essence of the Pedagogy.* Greenwich, CT: Information Age Publishing.
This collection of essays discusses critical theoretical and methodological issues in research on service learning in universities and K–12 schools, as well as factors that affect the sustainability of programs.

Maurasse, David. 2001. *Beyond the Campus: How Colleges and Universities Form Partnerships with Their Communities.* New York, NY: Routledge.
Based on in-depth case studies of four institutions across the broad spectrum of higher education (University of Pennsylvania, San Francisco State University, Xavier University, and Hostos Community College), this book offers great insight into institutional processes of reform in developing service-learning and university-community partnerships.

Sirianni, Carmen and Lewis A. Friedland. 2004. "The New Student Politics: Sustainable Action for Democracy," *Journal of Public Affairs* 7:1, 101–23.
This article examines recent efforts to reorient student civic engagement on campuses around a robust conception of relational politics and coproduction and compares these to the participatory democracy of student movements in the 1960s.

Stanton, Timothy K., Dwight E. Giles, and Nadinne Cruz. 1999. *Service Learning: A Movement's Pioneers Reflect on Its Origins, Practice, and Future.* San Francisco, CA: Jossey-Bass.
Through oral histories, this book looks at the early years of the service-learning movement in the United States through the eyes of its founding practitioners and sees social action as part of its core legacy that ought not to be lost with institutionalization.

Vidal, Avis, Nancy Nye, Christopher Walker, et al. 2002. *Lessons from the Community Outreach Partnership Center Program.* Washington, DC: Urban Institute.
This evaluation of the COPC program at the Office of University Partnerships, U.S. Department of Housing and Urban Development, explores the largely successful experiences of 25 university grantees and their community partners, especially nonprofit community-based organizations and neighborhood associations, and offers important

lessons for improving such partnerships and engaging in strategic community revitalization.

Zlotkowski, Edward. 1998. *Successful Service Learning Programs: New Models of Excellence in Higher Education.* Bolton, MA: Anker.

This important collection examines diverse service-learning and action-research models on 10 leading campuses in the service-learning movement from which we still have much to learn.

Community Youth Development and K-12 Civic Education

Billig, Shelley H. 2000. "Research on K–12 School-Based Service-Learning: The Evidence Builds," *Phi Delta Kappan* (May), 658–64.

This wide-ranging review of the research on service learning discusses some of the limits of existing research but notes the promising results in well-designed programs in terms of academic performance and personal development, as well as civic knowledge, attitudes, and engagement. It also discusses what practitioners see as the essential elements of good design. *On-line.*

Bradylyons, Morgan. 2002. *An Evaluation of the Boston-area Youth Organizing Project.* Honors thesis. Cambridge, MA: Harvard University, Committee on Degrees in Social Studies.

This senior honors thesis provides one of the few detailed accounts of youth organizing, in this case of an organization that draws largely on the faith-based organizing model.

Butts, Jeffrey A., Janeen Buck, and Mark B. Coggeshall. 2002. *The Impact of Teen Court on Young Offenders.* Washington, DC: The Urban Institute.

This evaluation of teen court programs in Alaska, Missouri, Maryland, and Arizona found significantly lower recidivism rates in two of them and raises questions for further research, especially on the greater efficacy of those with relatively higher youth participation and authority. Its discussion of theoretical propositions underlying youth courts' effectiveness is especially helpful.

Calvert, Matthew, Shepherd Zeldin, and Amy Weisenbach. 2002. *Youth Involvement for Community, Organizational, and Youth Development:*

Directions for Research, Evaluation, and Practice. Madison, WI: University of Wisconsin and Innovation Center for Community and Youth Development / Tides Center.

Following on an earlier study by Zeldin and colleagues on youth decision making, this report sketches further questions for research on skills, impact, policies, and the relation of the youth participation movement to other movements. *On-line.*

Checkoway, Barry. 1994. *Youth Participation in Neighborhood Development.* Washington, DC: Academy for Educational Development.

This influential report analyzes various strategies for actively involving young people in community development.

Delgado, Melvin. 2002. *New Frontiers for Youth Development in the 21st Century.* New York, NY: Columbia University Press.

This book provides an overview of the paradigm of mobilizing community and youth assets in the youth development field.

Dionne, E.J., Kayla Drogosz, and Robert Litan (eds.). 2003. *United We Serve: National Service and the Future of Citizenship.* Washington, DC: Brookings Institution.

This collection contains useful reflections by leading practitioners and scholars on the origins, practices, and politics of national and community service programs.

Galston, William A. 2001. "Political Knowledge, Political Engagement, and Civic Education," *Annual Review of Political Science* 4: 217–34.

This indispensable review of the literature argues that on a broad range of indicators civic knowledge does make a difference in enabling people to function as democratic citizens and that class-room-based civic education, as well as well-designed service learning, can provide important foundations.

Gimpel, James, J. Celeste Lay, and Jason Schuknecht. 2003. *Cultivating Democracy: Civic Environment and Political Socialization in America.* Washington, DC: Brookings Institution.

Based on interviews with a diverse sample of high school students, the authors explore school and other forms of political socialization and ways of promoting civic engagement for those most at risk of becoming nonparticipants.

Keeter, Scott, Cliff Zukin, Molly Andolina, and Krista Jenkins. 2002. *The Civic and Political Health of the Nation: A Generational Portrait*. College Park, MD: Center for Information and Research on Civic Learning and Engagement.

Based on a national telephone survey of 3,246 respondents, this revealing study examines the differences in civic and political partic- ipation of four generational cohorts (Matures, Baby Boomers, Generation X, and DotNets) and finds that younger cohorts hold their own in volunteering and community problem-solving activities but lag in electoral activities. Consumer activism appears as a rela- tively common activity, and those "dual activists" who engage in both civic and electoral work constitute 11 percent of youth ages 15–25, as compared to 16 percent of the general population.

Kirschner, Benjamin, Jennifer L. O'Donoghue, and Milbrey McLaughlin (eds.). 2002. *Youth Participation: Improving Institutions and Communities in New Directions for Youth Development (Winter)*. San Francisco, CA: Jossey-Bass.

This collection of articles reviews some of the limits of our knowl- edge about youth civic engagement, as well as some models of youth organizing, foundation strategy, and youth evaluation.

Lewis-Charp, Heather, Hanh Cao Yu, Sengsouvanh Soukamneuth, and Johanna Lacoe of Social Policy Research Associates. 2003. *Extending the Reach of Youth Development through Activism: Research Results from the Youth Leadership for Development Initiative. 2 volumes*. Takoma Park, MD: Innovation Center for Community and Youth Development.

This extensive evaluation of the five-year YLDI project, directed by the Innovation Center for Community and Youth Development and funded by the Ford Foundation, provides key insight into the leadership development, organizational dynamics, and youth devel- opment outcomes among the 11 participating organizations, which, unlike many other youth development programs, have either youth organizing or identity support among hard-to-reach older youth as their main focus.

McDonnell, Lorraine M., T. Michael Timpane, and Michael Benjamin
(eds.). 2000. *Rediscovering the Democratic Purposes of Education.*
Lawrence, KS: University of Kansas Press.

    The essays in this collection, which range from the normative and
historical to institutional and political, analyze why the democratic
purposes of schooling have remained on the periphery of educational reform. The essays also explore strategies for change.

Nessel, Paula A. 2000. *Youth Court: A National Movement.* Technical
Assistance Bulletin No. 17. Chicago, IL: American Bar Association,
Division for Public Education.

    This publication provides an overview of the growth of the
youth court movement and its infrastructure at the local, state,
and federal levels.

Niemi, Richard G. and Jane Junn. 1998. *Civic Education: What Makes
Students Learn?* New Haven, CT: Yale University Press.

    Based on an examination of the 1988 civics assessment data of the
National Assessment of Educational Progress, this study argues
that the school civics curriculum enhances student knowledge of
American government and politics and that a greater emphasis
on local politics (among other things) could further strengthen
civic education.

Sherrod, Lonnie, Constance Flanagan, and Ron Kassimir (eds.).
Forthcoming. *Youth Activism: An International Encyclopedia.* Westport,
CT: Greenwood Publishing.

    This encyclopedia contains a very broad range of entries and case
studies by leading scholars and practitioners from around the world.

Sirianni, Carmen. Forthcoming. "Civic Innovation and Youth
Engagement: The Hampton Model of Systems Change and Culture
Change," in Frank Fischer, Carmen Sirianni, and Michael Geppert
(eds.) *Critical Studies in Organization and Bureaucracy, third edition.*
Philadelphia, PA: Temple University Press.

    This article examines how youth civic engagement can become an
essential component of change on a citywide basis, including in key

departments of city government, the school system, and the leading youth development agency. A process of relational organizing is combined with reinventing government to produce one of the most robust youth engagement systems in the United States.

Villarruel, Francisco A., Daniel F. Perkins, Lynn M. Borden, and Joanne G. Keith (eds.). 2003. *Community Youth Development: Programs, Policies, and Practices.* Thousand Oaks, CA: Sage.

This collection provides an overview of research in the field, with topics ranging from minority and immigrant youth to professional development among youth workers and youth civic engagement.

Youniss, James and Miranda Yates. 1997. *Community Service and Social Responsibility in Youth.* Chicago, IL: University of Chicago Press.

This rich ethnographic study of a Catholic high school enrolling mostly middle-class African American students in Washington, D.C., shows how student civic identity can form through community service and service learning with an explicit social justice frame.

Healthy Communities

Emanuel, Ezekiel and Linda Emanuel. 1997. "Preserving Community in Health Care," *Journal of Health Politics, Policy, and Law* 22:1 (February), 147–84.

Two leading bioethicists explore the strengths and limits of community-based health care approaches, including democratic polity in managed care, and contrast the model of democratic accountability to economic and professional models.

Light, Donald. 1997. "The Rhetorics and Realities of Community Health Care: The Limits of Countervailing Powers to Meet the Health Care Needs of the Twenty-first Century," *Journal of Health Politics, Policy and Law* 22:2 (April), 105–45.

A leading medical sociologist examines the history of community-based approaches and their relative marginalization in the context of corporate restructuring and in comparison to current community innovations in several countries with long-established national health insurance.

Minkler, Meredith, Nina Wallerstein, and Budd Hall (eds.). 2002. *Community-Based Participatory Research for Health.* San Francisco, CA: Jossey-Bass.

This collection provides extensive analysis of theories, methods, and case studies of participatory research that links research, action, and education as part of a democratic collaborative process with community actors, especially on issues relating to health and community development.

Minkler, Meredith (ed.). 1997. *Community Organizing and Community Building for Health.* New Brunswick, NJ: Rutgers University Press.

Drawing on the convergence of various forms of community organizing, participatory action-research, and assets-based community building, this essay collection by leading scholars analyzes grassroots public health strategies and projects on a broad range of issues from HIV/AIDS and substance abuse to violence and environmental toxins.

Schlesinger, Mark, "Paradigms Lost: The Persisting Search for Community in U.S. Health Policy," *Journal of Health Politics, Policy and Law* 22:4 (Aug 1997), 937–92.

The author examines the history of community-based health approaches and qualified public support and concludes that their potential is linked to the reemergence of a more active federal government role in health care.

Public Journalism and Civic Communications

Bollier, David. 2002. *Silent Theft: The Private Plunder of Our Common Wealth.* New York, NY: Routledge.

The author argues that the regime of private property is appropriating common goods in domains ranging from natural resources and drug research to cyberspace. A comprehensive summary of many of the most important aspects of the commons movement.

Carey, James W. 1992. Dayton, OH: Kettering Foundation. "The Press and the Public Discourse." *Kettering Review* 9–22 (Winter).

This early statement stresses the necessity of rethinking the relationship of the press to the public in the tradition of John Dewey.

Delli Carpini, Michael X. 1998. *"Reframing News: Press Coverage of Public Journalism."* Dayton, OH: Kettering Foundation.
The author presents a comprehensive consideration of the most important arguments made against public journalism by its critics.

Friedland, Lewis A. 2003. *Public Journalism: Past and Future.* Dayton, OH: Kettering Foundation.
This book contains four in-depth case studies that examine how public journalism has transformed newsrooms and news routines while also exploring the limits of change.

Hess, Charlotte and Elinor Ostrom. 2003. "Ideas, Artifacts, and Facilities: Information as a Common-Pool Resource," *Law & Contemporary Problems* 66, 1–2 (Winter/Spring), 111–148.
The authors present a central argument that information is, indeed, a common-pool resource.

Kranich, Nancy. 2004. *The Information Commons: A Public Policy Report.* New York, NY: Free Expression Policy Project.
This excellent, comprehensive overview of both the core ideas of the information commons movement and the movement itself in its various forms provides the best starting point for anyone.

Lessig, Lawrence. 2001. *The Future of Ideas: The Fate of the Commons in a Connected World.* New York: Random House.
An intellectual leader of the commons movement argues that free intellectual production depends on an effective commons movement accompanied by new forms of common intellectual property.

Levine, Peter. 2000. "The Internet and Civil Society," *Philosophy and Public Policy* 20:1–8.
This important essay outlines the specific impacts that the Internet is likely to have on contemporary civil society and considers the relationship between local space and cyberspace.

Ostrom, Elinor. 1990. *Governing the Commons: The Evolution of Institutions for Collective Action.* New York, NY: Cambridge University Press.

This complex but central statement of the basic principles of common-pool resource governance, which counters the "tragedy of the commons" argument, has influenced virtually all writers on the information commons movement.

Rosen, Jay. 1999. *What Are Journalists For?* New Haven, CT: Yale University Press.

This book offers a comprehensive summary statement on the principles and achievements of the public journalism movement by one of its intellectual leaders.

Schudson, Michael. 1999. *"What Public Journalism Knows about Journalism but Doesn't Know about 'Public'."* In Theodore L. Glasser (ed.), *The Idea of Public Journalism.* New York, NY: Guilford Press.

One of America's leading scholars of the news offers criticism of the movement that recognizes its importance in the transformation of American journalism but argues that it does not go far enough.

Sirianni, Carmen, and Lewis A. Friedland. 2001. *Civic Innovation in America: Community Empowerment, Public Policy, and the Movement for Civic Renewal.* Berkeley: University of California Press.

Chapter 5 presents a comprehensive overview of the first decade of the civic journalism movement.

Index

R